SECOND EDITION

iPad in One Hour FOR LITIGATORS

TOM MIGHELL

D0905535

ABALAW
PRACTICE
DIVISION
The Business of Practicing Law

Cover design by RIPE Creative, Inc.

Library of Congress Cataloging-in-Publication Data

Mighell, Tom, author.
  iPad in one hour for litigators / by Tom Mighell. — Second Edition.
    pages cm
  Includes bibliographical references and index.
  ISBN 978-1-63425-062-7 (alk. paper)
  1. iPad (Computer) 2. Practice of law—United States—Data processing. 3. Lawyers—United States—Handbooks, manuals, etc. I. Title.
  KF320.A9M48   2015
  004.1675—dc23

                                                                    2015003270

Contents

About the Author

 **Tom Mighell** is a Senior Consultant with Contoural, Inc., where he helps companies develop information governance, litigation readiness, and privacy programs. Prior to becoming a consultant, Tom practiced as a trial lawyer for 18 years with the firm of Cowles & Thompson in Dallas. He served as the firm's Litigation Technology Support Coordinator for six years, running the technology for lawyers in more than 50 trials.

Tom is the author of *iPad in One Hour for Lawyers, iPad Apps in One Hour for Lawyers*, and the coauthor (along with Dennis Kennedy) of *The Lawyer's Guide to Collaboration Tools and Technologies: Smart Ways to Work Together*, all published by the American Bar Association. Tom publishes the legal technology blog Inter Alia (www.inter-alia.net), and is also the cohost of The Kennedy-Mighell Report, a legal technology podcast (via www.legaltalknetwork.com).

Tom has been a member of the ABA's Law Practice Division since 2003. During that time he served for four years on the ABA TECH-SHOW Board and as the chair of ABA TECHSHOW 2008. He served as chair of the Law Practice Division from 2011 through 2012 and currently serves as the chair of the Section's Publishing Board. Tom received both his B.A. (1987) and J.D. (1990) degrees from The University of Texas at Austin.

Acknowledgments

To Denise in LP Books—for all your hard work and dedication to publishing great law practice management books; to the LP Publishing Board, who are among the hardest-working volunteers in the Division; to the wonderful trial lawyers and judges who contributed their thoughts and experiences to this book, for providing some invaluable information for those interested in using the iPad in the courtroom; and to Kenny, who patiently looks the other way when I *have* to buy the latest iPad, for "book research" purposes . . .

Introduction

When the iPad was introduced five years ago, it was viewed almost exclusively as a device for content consumption. As lawyers started to use the tablet in their practices, we found the iPad could also serve as a productivity tool, and make it easier or more convenient for us to accomplish a lot of the work we do every day. Although the iPad won't necessarily make you a better lawyer, there's no question that it can make you a more productive lawyer, which can improve the service you provide to your clients.

It didn't take long before trial lawyers were experimenting with the iPad in court. Apps began to appear that were specifically designed for casework, including trials and hearings. The number of lawyers using iPads at trial is increasing all the time, as more and more litigators learn how well suited the device is for the courtroom.

When I talk to lawyers on this topic, they typically ask these questions more than any others:

Can I try a case with my iPad? Yes, definitely. In this book, I'll show you how to get started.

Can I try *all* my cases with my iPad? Maybe, but the better question is, "*Should* I try all my cases with my iPad?" Although the iPad is a remarkable device to use in the courtroom, it might not lend itself to every case you have. An iPad's storage capacity can certainly hold large volumes of documents—just 20GB of storage can hold over 700,000 pages of PDF files, which translates to almost 300 standard file boxes! What is less clear, however, is how the applications ("apps") you want to use in trial will perform with large numbers of documents. Further, although current trial presentation apps are fairly full-featured, in some cases you may need additional features, which as of this writing are only in the desktop versions of Trial Director, Sanction, and other Windows-based trial presentation software packages.

Does it matter which model iPad I have? Yes. The newer your iPad, the faster and more powerful it is going to be. Also, a more recent model will allow you to take advantage of apps that are updated with the latest features—features that might not work as well on an earlier model. Although Apple has released five models since 2010, at the time of this writing, only three models are available for sale. Here are my thoughts on the trial-worthiness of all iPad models:

iPad Version	Suitability for Trial
1st Generation (iPad 1)	Not recommended. Although AirPlay can be enabled, it is complicated, and the iPad is not strong enough to mirror evidence presentation apps.
2nd Generation (iPad 2)	Suitable for trial presentation, but this model is starting to get a little old.
3rd Generation ("the New iPad")	Not recommended. iOS 8 is not compatible with this model.
iPad with Retina Display (4th Generation)	Suitable for trial presentation
iPad Air and iPad Air 2	Suitable for trial presentation
iPad Mini 2 and 3	Good as a content consumption or note-taking device in the courtroom, but more difficult to use for evidence presentation.

My firm uses litigation support tools such as Summation, CaseMap, and Relativity to prepare for trial; can I use them with the iPad? At the time of this writing, no. None of these popular litigation support tools offers an iPad companion app. But I expect that to change; as you'll read later, Trial Director now offers an iPad app, which allows you to create a case in the desktop version and transfer it to your tablet for presentation in the courtroom. More and more legal technology companies are developing iPad-ready versions of their software, so keep checking back—they may eventually develop an app for the tool you like. Most companion apps are free because you're already paying for the desktop version.

Will using the iPad in court make a difference with the judge or jury? Will it make me more persuasive in their eyes? Maybe. But maybe not. Most jurors these days expect to see lawyers using some type of technology in the courtroom, and the lawyers I know who have used the iPad at trial report the jury being impressed with the way technology helps them present their case. But you shouldn't count on that and use an iPad solely to impress a jury. No matter what technology you use at trial, your only responsibility is to use it properly; the only certainty is that if you *don't*, you won't score any points with the judge *or* jury.

For the structure of this book, I have imagined a new lawsuit for your office—*Marvin Davis v. ACME Industries, Inc.* The lessons will progress through the life cycle of the case:

- Initial case intake and docketing (Lesson 1)
- Conducting discovery—reviewing documents and taking depositions (Lesson 2)
- Preparing for trial by making sure you have the right technology equipment (Lesson 3)
- Conducting legal research about your case before trial, in hearings, or during the trial itself (Lesson 4)

- Selecting a jury without having to use your legal pad (Lesson 5)
- Presenting evidence to a judge or jury (Lesson 6)

At the end I'll provide insight from trial lawyers who use the iPad in court every day, including some great tips for making sure everything goes smoothly when you take your tablet to trial.

Finally, a Few Notes Before We Get Started

The Illusion of "One Hour." Although this is a "One Hour" book, you may find it takes you a little more than an hour to read. It will certainly take you more than an hour to try out all the apps I mention in the book. One of the great challenges of a book of this nature is finding the right place to cut off the flow of information; I hope I have provided you enough without leaving too many questions. If you'd like to continue the conversation, feel free to contact me any time at my blog, Inter Alia (http://www.inter-alia.net).

I May Not Recommend All the Apps I Mention. There are a few apps in this book that I mention but do not recommend. Why is that? It's primarily to show you what application developers are trying to achieve in the area of trial and litigation. You'll read about some very innovative ideas that developers are bringing to the App Store, but the execution may be less than ideal. The app may not be ready for prime time yet, but it might be in the future. Or another app may come out that perfectly nails the concept. Get educated on the possibilities here, and then be patient.

A Note about Change. On the iPad, things can change very quickly. Apps may have new features, while others may have been removed; a button that was on the left in an older version may have been moved to the right. For certain apps, the features described in this book may be unavailable by the time you read the book. Likewise, new features may have debuted that correct particular issues I mention here. The price of the app may change, as the developer may occasionally put the app on sale or increase the cost to test a higher price point. Indeed, the app itself may go away completely, or the developer may simply stop supporting it. To keep up with the latest developments, follow me at Inter Alia (http://www.inter-alia.net), where I review new apps, discuss changes to current apps, and provide tips on how to get the most out of your device.

The iPad and Legal-Specific Apps. One interesting development since the publication of the first edition of this book in 2013: a lot of the legal-specific apps mentioned in the book have not been updated—at all. Even more striking, some of the apps mentioned in the first edition have been *completely removed* from the App Store, which of course means I can't recommend or include them in this edition. Typically, when a developer stops updating an app, it's not a great sign for the app's future utility. Although these apps will continue to work (for a time, anyway; eventually, a new version of iOS will come along that may render the older app unusable), they will never get better, or have new features, or fix old features that needed fixing. So while I won't necessarily tell you not to use these outdated apps, be prepared for the day when the app no longer works. You have been warned.

Ready? Let's go!

A New Case—
Managing Details and Deadlines

A new lawsuit has been filed—*Marvin Davis v. ACME Industries, Inc.* For the purposes of this book, it won't matter whether your client is the plaintiff or the defendant. You no doubt already have a checklist of the steps you ordinarily take to protect your client's interests: file appropriate complaints or answers, make sure relevant documents are preserved, and understand where the case is filed and who is on the other side, among many other things. Now that you have an iPad, you can also ask yourself: Can the iPad help me with any of this?

For lawsuits in general, the answer is a solid "*yes*." As we'll discuss throughout this book, many apps can help you with certain aspects of the litigation process. However, in some areas, app availability will be a little leaner than in others; further, in other areas, apps that were recommended years ago haven't been updated. In this lesson, we'll discuss the apps you might use during the case intake process, from gathering information about the claims or defenses to making sure you have appropriately calendared the relevant deadlines.

Gathering Case Information

Whether you represent the plaintiff or the defendant, at some point your client comes in to meet with you, and you need a way to record that information. The iPad is an ideal data input device for either handwritten or typewritten notes. Here are some examples of apps that can get you started.

Note-taking

For many lawyers, the iPad has replaced the traditional legal pad, both in and out of the courtroom. Lawyers now use the iPad regularly to take notes during meetings, mediations, hearings, or at trial. If you prefer handwriting notes to typing them, there are dozens of note-taking apps that can help you. For my money, the following are the best apps for writing notes.

Noteshelf (http://bit.ly/1xnfi1O) is my favorite note-taking app, hands down. It's really simple to set up and organize your notebooks; you can organize them by client, by case, or in any other format you prefer. When you open Noteshelf, you'll notice the handy bookshelf layout, with a display of all your notes (see Figure 1.1a).

To get started, just press the **+** sign in the upper right to create a new notebook. Select **_Quick Create_** for a default style, or **_Customize Notebook_** to select your own paper and cover. Tap at the top to add a title, and press **_Create_**.

Figure 1.1a Noteshelf

Make sure you turn on the zoom function before you start writing; in my opinion, it's the most important feature of any note-taking app. In fact, no matter which note-taking app you choose, my advice is to make sure it offers a zoom feature. Without it, your handwriting will be overly large on the page, and you'll end up using many more pages than you expect.

The zoom feature shrinks your handwriting so you can fit much more text onto each page. With Noteshelf, you can configure the zoom factor as well as the line spacing to make sure your notes end up exactly where you want them (see Figure 1.1b).

Figure 1.1b Noteshelf with Zoom Feature

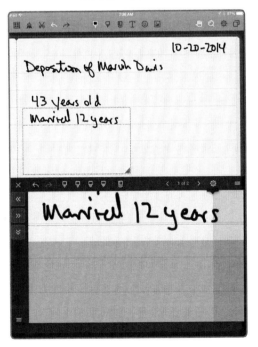

Noteshelf offers multiple pen types and highlighters in several colors, an eraser, and the ability to insert text, images, or emoticons into your notes. When you have finished taking notes, they are saved within Noteshelf, or you can export them in PDF or JPEG format. You can also email your notebooks to others, or save them to Dropbox, Box, Google Drive, Evernote, or a photo album.

As mentioned before, there are many great note-taking apps—too many to mention in a one-hour book. Following are two more I recommend.

Notability (http://bit.ly/1ob6jhY) is not only a good note-taking app, it's one of the best for making an audio recording of a meeting, deposition, or other event for which you are taking notes. Even better, Notability will synchronize the audio with your handwritten or typewritten notes. Let's say that following the initial meeting with your client, you find that your notes on a particular item aren't as clear as you would like. With Notability, you can simply press that area of your notes to hear the audio of what was recorded at that exact time; you don't have to listen to the entire recording. When you're done, you can forward your notes with audio via email to yourself or anyone you choose, or save them to a Dropbox, Google Drive, or Box account.

If you prefer text to handwriting, check out **WritePad Pro** (http://bit. ly/1qLSbwm), which has a nice handwriting recognition engine that will convert your scribbles to text. The app tries to predict what it is you're trying to write, so you can just press the correct word(s) to enter them on the document above and save yourself a few pen strokes. Your sharing options are more limited, in that you are only able to export to PDF, email as HTML, or share via Twitter or Facebook.

Documents and Text Files

Some lawyers are better at keyboarding than writing by hand, and so might find note-taking apps a bit cumbersome. If that describes you, then you will probably feel most comfortable with a document creation or text editing app. If you are a Microsoft Office user, your best option is **Microsoft Word for iPad** (http://bit.ly/1e17n4j), which allows you to create and revise Word documents easily on your tablet. You can save documents to a Microsoft OneDrive account or Dropbox. You'll need an Office 365 subscription (about $100/year; visit http://bit.ly/1Gd0pDo for more information) to enjoy full features of the app; I use Office 365 and can definitely recommend it. You can still use the Word app to edit documents on your iPad without a subscription, but the features are more limited.

If the cost of the Office 365 subscription is too steep, then try **Documents to Go** (http://bit.ly/1m3PB4r). It offers probably the best conversion of Office documents on the iPad, and the one-time fee of $16.99 is definitely cheaper than a subscription to Office 365. On the other hand, you won't find all the bells and whistles of the original Microsoft applications. It's a solid tool, however, for basic creation and editing of Word documents.

If all you need to do is put words down on a virtual sheet of paper, a basic text editor may be all you need. Like the note-taking apps above, there are dozens of apps that are great for simple text entry. My recommended favorites are **Editorial** (http://bit.ly/1D537Kt), **Drafts** (http://bit.ly/1siykCu), and **Nebulous Notes** (http://bit.ly/1oHKBhG). All of these are great for taking simple notes and saving them as text files or to a Dropbox account later on.

Case Intake Apps

Maybe all you need to do during the initial meetings with your client is take notes about the new case; however, you might need an app that does more than that—one that helps you collect information on a more powerful level. If you have a routine intake procedure for all of your cases, or a certain type of case, take a look at **FormConnect** (http://bit.ly/1tO03Mi). It allows you to create virtually any form you like for data entry. You can design an intake form with fields for text, the date, check boxes, drop-down menus, radio buttons, labels, signature lines, images, or notes. To design your form, simply take one of the elements from the box and drag it anywhere on the form. You can then label it, select a font size, and customize it in other ways, and then place and size it on the form exactly as you want (see Figure 1.2).

Figure 1.2 FormConnect Design Screen

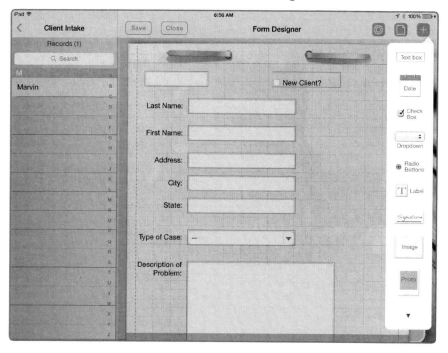

Once you design your form, you can tab from field to field as you enter data during the interview. Your data is stored in a database, and you can export that data in a variety of formats, including PDF, CSV, XML, or HTML. You can email the information to yourself or others, file it in a Dropbox folder, or open it in another iPad app. FormConnect is an ideal choice for lawyers who gather the same type of information for each case; you can set up as many forms as you like for different types of cases or clients.

For an all-in-one client intake solution, try **Clipboard PDF Pro** (http://bit.ly/1uAWTgH), an app that combines a number of data-gathering tools in one place. You'll need to do a bit of preparation ahead of time—namely, create PDF versions of the intake forms you want to use. (It's easy to create a fillable PDF form if you have the right tools; unfortunately, the "how-to" for that is beyond the scope of this book. Adobe offers a video tutorial for Acrobat users at http://adobe.ly/1s1aG2i.)

The forms you create could include a basic client information form, medical or other release, a retainer agreement, or even forms that list specific information about the client's case. Once you have created the PDF forms you want, you'll need to load them into the app via email. Send the documents to yourself, and then use the ***Open In . . .*** option in email to move the files into the app. They will reside in your Master Forms list, so you can use them over and over again (see Figure 1.3).

Figure 1.3 Using Clipboard PDF Pro for Case Intake

To start, create a folder for your case, on the left. Then choose a form you have created. Open it and begin filling it out as you gather information from your client. There's a pen button in the upper left that, when pressed, allows you or your client to sign anywhere on the PDF form. The document can then be saved to your intake folder.

The app is not limited to PDF forms, however. You can also add photographs, notes, and even create audio recordings for your intake folder. I like that you can have all of your intake information in one location, no matter the format. Without Clipboard Pro PDF, you would need a couple of different apps (or maybe just GoodReader—see below) to accomplish all of these data collection tasks. You can also email all of your client's information in a folder to yourself or others, so you can store it in other locations if you prefer to keep it outside of your iPad. The app is fairly basic, but it definitely gets the job done.

Docketing and Related Apps

One of the first things you'll do after filing a lawsuit is calendar the appropriate deadlines for the type of case and your jurisdiction. You might use sophisticated docketing software to track the deadlines, or simply calculate the deadlines yourself and enter individual appointments into your Outlook or other calendar. If you fall into the latter category, or you aren't using any tool to manage court deadlines, you might consider using an iPad app to help out at this stage of the case.

Interestingly, this is one area in which app developers seem to have lost interest since the last edition of this book—none of the apps described below have been updated in quite some time. This does not mean that they are completely useless, however; as long as you accept the possibility that they may never be updated again, these apps do have some utility.

The app that provides the most flexibility is one that doesn't rely on online updates, and that's **Court Days Pro** (http://bit.ly/1qViqkg). This app gives you the ability to enter your own deadlines (see Figure 1.4). It may take a little time to set these rules up, but you'll have them forever once they are entered.

Figure 1.4 Court Days Pro

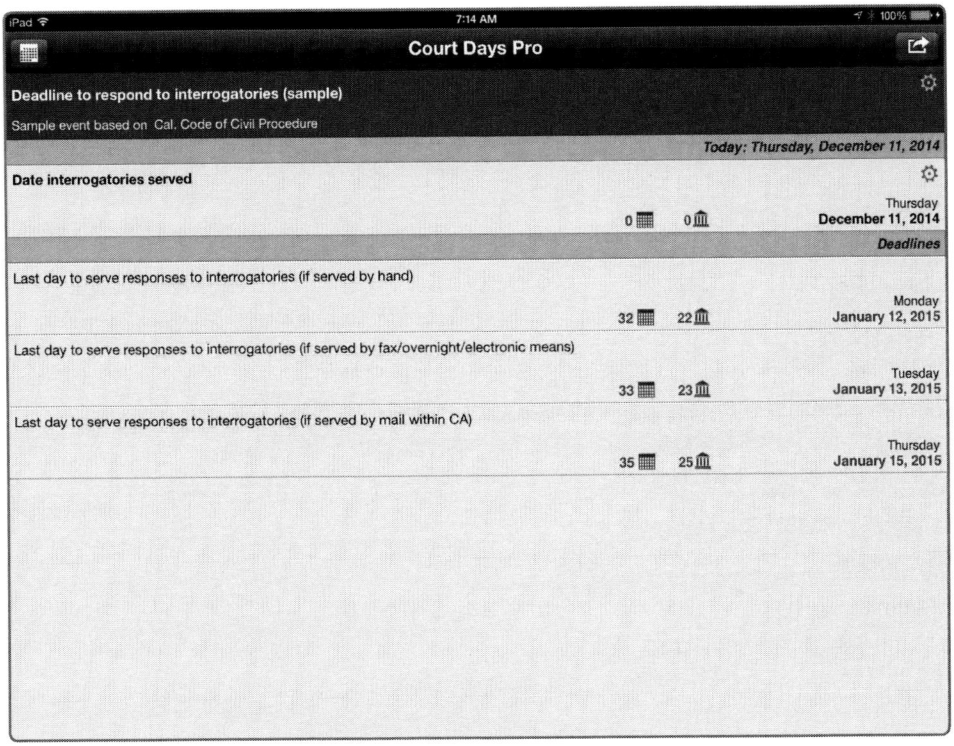

You are able to add dates directly to your iPad's calendar from the app, or email them to yourself or your client; if you use the email option, you'll need to enter deadlines on the calendar yourself. The ability to enter and save deadlines from your own jurisdiction makes this app pretty useful, despite the fact that it might never be updated with new features. This manual entry makes it potentially more valuable than the following apps, which rely on online services to update the calendaring rules.

One of these apps is **Smart Dockets** (http://bit.ly/1BHA666), which is free. To use the app, you'll have to register for an account. Once you log in, you'll be prompted to select a Court Rule Set. The list is very long, somewhat confusing to follow, and, unfortunately, incomplete. It includes courts and rules from all 50 states, but not all the rules. To find a rule set for your case, begin keying in your jurisdiction to narrow down the list.

Next, enter the trigger type—again, the list can be long and unorganized, but you can use the search function here, too. Fill out the other optional information and press **Generate Events**. (There's also a **Quick Date Calculator** button you can press if you just need a single deadline calculated.)

On the next screen, you'll see a listing of all the deadlines that apply to the designated trigger event (see Figure 1.5). Move **Authoritative**

Figure 1.5 Smart Dockets

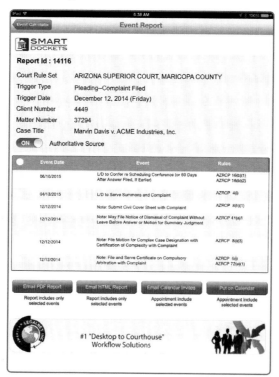

Source to *ON* so you can see the rules from which the deadlines are taken. You can then generate a report of these deadlines in three different formats: HTML, PDF, or via email. No matter which option you choose, you cannot view it on your iPad—it will be sent to you via email. If you choose the *Email Calendar Invites* option, you'll get an email with calendar invites attached for each of the calculated deadlines. Just double-click them and press *Save* to create an event in Outlook or other calendar program. You can also just press *Put on Calendar* to add to your iPad's calendar.

Smart Dockets is a great app and is worth trying out because it is free. However, as of this writing, the app has not been updated since 2012. This doesn't mean that the calendar deadlines are out of date, because the service provides that information online, not necessarily within the app. You should always make sure the developer is still supporting the app by updating its content.

In terms of features and ease of use, **DocketLaw** (http://bit.ly/1nVjjUZ) is another great app. However, since it also hasn't been updated in a long time and relies on an online subscription for access to calendaring rules, I'm not sure it's as good as Court Days Pro or Smart Dockets.

DocketLaw is an iPhone/iPad-only service that currently calculates deadlines for 28 states, although for some of those states it only provides rules for certain federal courts. Let's say you want to calculate deadlines for the discovery cutoff in federal court. Just select from a number of triggers and enter the date (as well as time and service type, if applicable). You'll see a listing of all deadlines under the Federal Rules of Civil Procedure. To see more detail on a particular deadline, just press it.

Like Smart Dockets, DocketLaw doesn't keep all the information to itself. Press the *Share* button and you'll find two options. Press *Add Events to Calendar* and all the deadlines will be exported to your iPad's calendar; if you sync with Exchange or another calendar program, all your deadlines will soon appear on your primary calendar. If you want to send the deadlines to your client, another attorney in your firm, or others, press *Email Events*, select the events you want to send, add a description, and press *Email Selected Events*.

The app also has a date calculator, which provides a simple way to count the number of calendar or court days from a particular date. All deadlines are kept updated by the service, and each court has holidays scheduled through the end of 2049. DocketLaw works on a subscription basis; depending on the jurisdiction, you could find yourself paying between $9.95 and $49.95 a month for this service.

For those of you in firms using CourtAlert (www.courtalert.com), there's a companion **CaseToGo** (http://bit.ly/1EmyiPl) app that allows you to download case information, including docket text, diaries, and related PDF files, to your iPad.

The last date calculator I'll mention is pretty average as a deadline calculator, but extremely useful for calculating lots of other things. **The Lawyer's Professional Assistant** (http://bit.ly/1wy7H2f) takes advantage of Wolfram|Alpha's powerful "computational knowledge engine" to bring you data on a wide range of topics useful to lawyers. You'll find more than 30 calculators and information sources in the following categories:

- Reference
- Calendar Computations
- Financial Computations
- Investigative Information
- Damages Determination
- Estate Planning
- Real Estate
- International

Using one of the calculators, it's a snap to determine the life expectancy of Marvin Davis, a 43-year-old (see Figure 1.6).

Figure 1.6 Lawyer's Professional Assistant

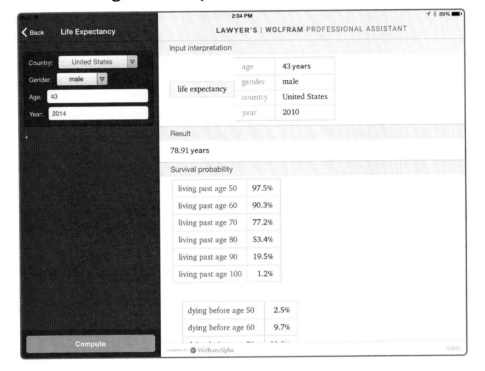

The number and breadth of calculators offered by this app makes it pretty much a no-brainer to have, whether or not you're using it for litigation.

By now you have met with your client, learned their side of the case, filed all appropriate pleadings, and calculated the relevant court deadlines. Now it's time to conduct discovery, so let's get started by heading to Lesson 2.

Discovery—
Documents and Depositions

Now that you have started to really dig in to the details of *Davis v. ACME Industries*, you're finding that both your client and the other side have a lot of relevant documents that must be gathered and reviewed. Medical records, expert reports, product-testing documents—the discovery phase of any lawsuit easily can result in the production of thousands of pages of documents, if not more. Fortunately, the iPad is a great tool for keeping track of case files, reviewing documents, and organizing exhibits for trial. In this lesson, we'll take a look at the apps I recommend for managing and reviewing case documents, as well as taking and annotating depositions.

Getting Electronic Documents onto Your iPad

First, though, let's answer what is probably the most important question for this lesson: How do you get documents onto the iPad in the first place? It's a good question, and I'll give the standard lawyer answer—*it depends*. You can move files onto your iPad in a number of ways, depending upon your preferences and how you plan to use the documents.

Document-sharing service. The most common way to get documents onto your iPad is by using a document-sharing service such as Dropbox (www.dropbox.com), Box (www.box.com), SugarSync (www.sugarsync.com), or SpiderOak (www.spideroak.com). I prefer Dropbox because it integrates with most of the apps I recommend in this book, and it's a great service. For instructions on how to set up one of these accounts (using Dropbox as an example), see Beyond the Lessons on page 112.

Dedicated server. Instead of using a commercial cloud-based service, you may decide to set up your own "personal cloud," or download files to your iPad via a dedicated server. Bigger law firms are starting to create their own document-sharing "services" by setting up servers with a direct connection to the lawyer's iPad. Some of these server types include WebDAV (Web Distributed Authoring and Versioning), FTP (File Transfer Protocol), SFTP (Secure File Transfer Program), AFP (Apple Filing Protocol), and SMB (Server Message Blog). You can configure apps such as GoodReader (see below) to work with servers like these, so you can download files directly with a greater level of security.

But you really don't need your own IT Department or fancy dedicated server to set up your own private cloud. Personal cloud storage is fairly affordable, and one of my favorite tools is the **Transporter** (www.filetransporter.com/). It's a hardware device that sits on your desk, with its own hard drive. Just plug it in and connect to your Internet service, then download and install the desktop software—just like you would with Dropbox or other cloud services. The Transporter connects wirelessly to any computer with the software installed, and you're accessing documents "in the cloud"—when in reality the files are right there on your desk.

Best of all, there are no monthly subscription fees as with other cloud services. You just pay for the hardware itself, at prices ranging from $99 to $349, depending on the size of the hard drive you select. It's a great option if you want to access your files from anywhere but would feel a bit more secure with those files under your own control.

Email. If you don't want to use a cloud-based service or file-server option, you can always email documents to yourself, and then open the attachment in the app of your choice. Once you've sent an email to yourself, open the message on your iPad and press on the attachment. You'll see a box like the one shown in Figure 2.1.

At the top, you can use AirDrop to instantly share the file with another iPad or iPhone user nearby. If someone's device is available, it will appear in that space. You'll see a row of all the apps currently installed on your iPad that you might use to view the attachment (see Figure 2.1); just navigate to the app you want, and the file will open up in that app. You will also see an option to ***Print*** (for use with an AirPrint-enabled printer) or to

Figure 2.1 Opening Email Attachments on an iPad

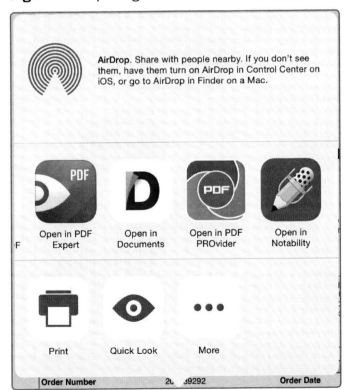

Security and Cloud-Based File Management

When I talk to lawyers about the iPad and mention Dropbox, I am invariably asked the question, "Is Dropbox secure?" The short answer is yes, but with a qualification.

Unlike other cloud file services, Dropbox provides only a single encryption key for your data; other companies provide you with your own encryption key, so you retain ultimate control over your data. Dropbox says the reason its employees need access to your encryption key is to provide you with better service should you need support, and this is probably true. Dropbox further states it has very strict access controls that prohibit employee access to user data, and the chances that a Dropbox employee would access your information are likely extremely low. **Note:** If you plan to store health or other records that might be covered by HIPAA, understand that Dropbox is not HIPAA-compliant. Use one of the other cloud services mentioned instead, or only use Dropbox to store nonconfidential records.

Nevertheless, you may wish to take precautions to guard against any possibility that confidential client information might be accessed. One option is to use tools such as Box or SpiderOak, which give you complete control over your encryption key. However, because Dropbox is connected to just about any app worth using on the iPad, I still recommend it. If, however, you are still concerned about whether storing confidential information in Dropbox is secure, here are some ways you can protect yourself and still use Dropbox:

- First, do not upload any documents or files you consider to be confidential to your main Dropbox folder. You can still use Dropbox for all of your other, nonconfidential files, if you like. Alternatively, use Dropbox as a transfer tool of confidential information. Use the service to transfer files to your iPad, then delete them from the Dropbox folder. The files will remain secure once they are on the iPad.
- For confidential files, use either **Viivo** (http://viivo.com/) or **Box-Cryptor** (www.boxcryptor.com) to provide an extra layer of security. These products will encrypt your confidential files within Dropbox, so only you have access to them. Both tools offer iPad apps—Viivo at http://bit.ly/1AXNJff and BoxCryptor at http://bit.ly/1wMoWvV.

take a ***Quick Look*** at the document without leaving the email. You now also have the ability to attach the file to a separate message for mailing to someone else by pressing on the ***Mail*** button, which will be one of your first options when the dialog box appears.

The biggest downside to moving documents onto your iPad using email is that it must be done one attachment at a time. With services like Dropbox or the Transporter, you can move entire folders of documents onto the iPad at once, which makes it much more efficient and convenient. Still, the email method is best for those of you with security concerns about cloud-based file-sharing services.

File Sharing in iTunes. Another way to move files onto your tablet in bulk is through File Sharing in iTunes. Here's how to do it:

- Connect the iPad to your computer.
- Launch iTunes (you must be using iTunes 9.1 or greater to take advantage of File Sharing).
- Once iTunes connects, click on the iPad button.
- Click the ***Apps*** button on the menu across the top to see all of the apps currently installed on your device.
- Scroll down below the apps to the section marked File Sharing. There you will see a list of all the applications that support File Sharing, including (hopefully) the one you want for your case files.
- Click on the application into which you want to move files.
- You can move files in one of two ways:
  - Click the ***Add*** button, which will bring up a dialog box that allows you to select the files you want to add.
  - Simply drag and drop your files, or even entire folders, directly onto the Documents list from the folder on your computer.

Using the File Sharing option in iTunes is good for the bulk movement of documents onto your iPad; however, to do it you will need to be connected to your computer, while the other two methods can be accomplished with a wireless connection. You can do this either by connecting the iPad to your computer or by enabling the Wireless Sync feature in Settings.

Scanning Paper Documents to Your iPad

What if, instead of providing you with electronic documents, your client or the other side provides you with paper records? If you already have a process established in your practice for scanning paper to PDF or TIFF files, then there's no need to change that process; simply scan the documents and move them onto your iPad using one of the methods described above. If, however, you don't have such a process, or you happen to be at your client's office and someone hands you a few records you'd like to quickly scan, why not use a scanning app to move the documents directly onto your iPad?

Just search for "document scanner" in the App Store, and you'll be presented with dozens of options. I'll mention two apps that I can recommend for all your scanning needs. The first is **Scanner Pro** (http://bit. ly/1q9B3fT). When you open the app, the layout and options are very simple; you can either take a picture of something you want to scan, or use an image that's already in your Photo Library.

For example, to scan your client's handwritten notes of a conversation he had with the other side, press the camera button to activate your iPad's camera. Once you take a picture of the page, you'll have the option to define the borders of the document yourself or to select the entire image. You can also specify the paper size of the document you're scanning as Letter, Legal, Ledger, Business Card, Tabloid, A3/A4/A5, or you can set up a custom size. Press **Done**, and you'll go to a page where you can adjust the brightness and contrast, rotate the document, and select between Photo, Document, or Grayscale. Press **Done** again, and your scan is complete. If you have a multipage document, just press the multipage button before you take a picture of the first page, and you can scan as many pages as you want.

When you're finished scanning, press the ***Actions*** button at the upper right, and you have a number of different options: emailing or printing the scanned document; uploading it to Dropbox, Evernote, Google Drive, iCloud, or a WebDAV server; or opening it as a PDF or JPEG in another app on your iPad. The high quality of the scans, as well as the sharing actions, make Scanner Pro a valuable app to own.

One thing that Scanner Pro *can't* do, however, is apply **OCR**, or Optical Character Recognition, to your document. If you want to be able to annotate the document in a PDF app or search it for terms relevant to your case, you are going to want an app that offers OCR capability. **PDFpen Scan+** (http://bit.ly/1AWQ7Z1) is such an app. It works much the same as Scanner Pro. You take a picture of all the pages you plan to scan, then press the ***OCR*** button. Crop the image if necessary, press ***OCR*** again, and the app will scan the images for all the words on it. When you're done, you can email the document, open it up in other iPad apps, or share to a number of cloud locations, including Dropbox, Evernote, Google Drive, Transporter, WebDAV, and FTP. OCR is a technology that is not always the most accurate, so you might see some errors. However, the quality is generally pretty good if you want to create searchable documents on your iPad.

Organizing and Reviewing Documents

By now you should have decided on your preferred method of moving documents to your iPad and have all of these files ready to go. Your next question is quite likely, How do I manage and review these files? Unlike your Windows- or Mac-based computers, the iPad does not come with a traditional folder structure for managing your files. Fortunately, many apps offer similar functionality and can provide most of what you need to organize case files. For me, the must-have app in this area, and one of the first apps all new iPad owners should purchase, is **GoodReader** (http://bit.ly/1reOU8Q).

The app offers an intuitive interface for managing your documents, with the main screen showing a "My Documents" list on the left and file management tools on the right (see Figure 2.2a). It's very simple to set up a folder for the *Davis v. ACME Industries* matter, as well as any other case or project you want to load on your iPad.

Figure 2.2a GoodReader

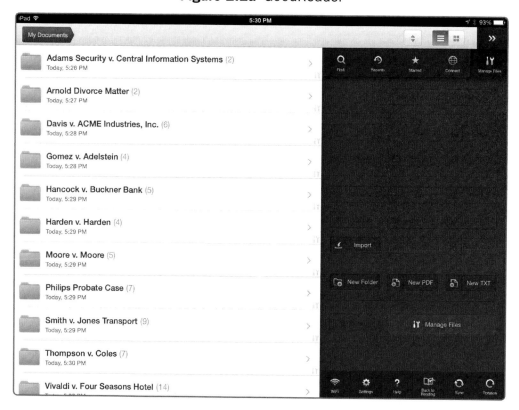

To set up your folders, press ***Manage Files*** on the right, and then press the ***New Folder*** button. Give your folder a name, and you're all set—or you can create subfolders within the original top-level folder. You can then download documents directly into your folders through one or more connections. GoodReader offers access to:

- Dropbox
- OneDrive
- Google Drive
- SugarSync
- Box
- WebDAV Server
- FTP Server
- SFTP Server
- AFP Server
- SMB Server
- Most online mail servers, as well as IMAP and POP3.

In addition to file management, GoodReader is also a pretty good app for reviewing documents, as if its name didn't give that away. You can view just about any kind of document you have—office documents (MS Office and iWork suites), PDFs, images (JPEG, TIFF, GIF), and audio and video files are all supported. Reviewing documents in GoodReader is easy. Just press on the document name and you'll be taken to the reading area. If you want to mark up the documents you're reviewing, they will need to be in PDF format (see Figure 2.2b). At the time of this writing, no document app, GoodReader included, can annotate any other type of document.

Figure 2.2b Annotating PDFs in GoodReader

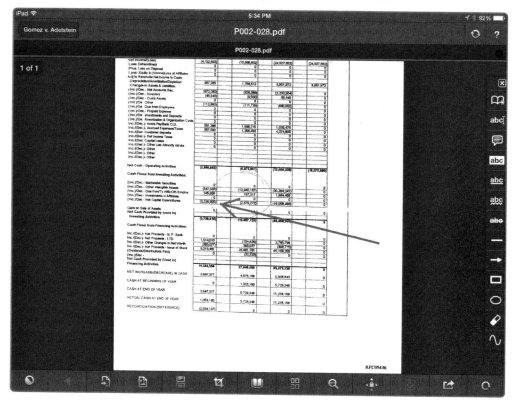

If you are dealing only with PDF files, you might want to load them all into a PDF annotation app for review. My favorite is **PDF Expert** (http://bit.ly/1ra1wjz), which also allows you to create folders for all of your cases (see Figure 2.3a).

PDF Expert offers a solid annotation feature set—everything a lawyer would need to mark up a document. You can add a box, circle, line, or arrow; highlight, underline, or cross out text; add comments; insert stamps

Figure 2.3a PDF Expert

(including exhibit stamps you create yourself); add text; and write on the document with your finger or a stylus (see Figure 2.3b). You can also edit a PDF just like a regular text document.

In addition to the annotation tools, I also like that PDF Expert supports fillable PDF forms, and it provides a dead simple way to sign PDF files (see Figure 2.3c). It's a good option when you have clients sign documents, because they can then be saved and forwarded to the court, opposing counsel, experts, or others.

Figure 2.3b
Annotation Tools
in PDF Expert

Figure 2.3c Signature Page in PDF Expert

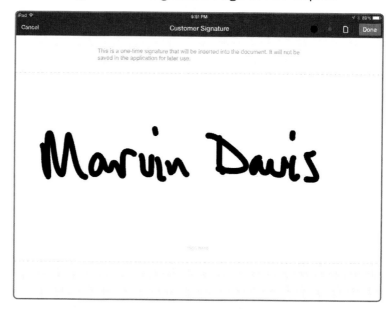

Although GoodReader and PDF Expert are my document management tools of choice for the iPad, there are many more apps worth a look. Two PDF apps I also recommend are **iAnnotate PDF** (http://bit.ly/1qhIr86) and **PDFpen** (http://bit.ly/1obDPAL). Both of these apps have similar functionality and do a great job helping you work with PDF files.

So far, we have only discussed document review apps that require you to load the files yourself; these work best if you have only a limited number of documents, or if you use cloud services such as Dropbox or Box for bigger cases to move files in bulk to the iPad. If your case deals with significantly more documents, your options are slightly more limited. It appears that eDiscovery vendors do not have a lot of interest in providing document review apps for mobile devices; instead, many vendors provide a "mobile-friendly" website where you can review documents using a browser such as Safari or Chrome.

One eDiscovery vendor that offers a mobile document review platform is Daegis, with its **Daegis Mobile** tool (http://www.daegis.com/technology/daegis-mobile/). The web app allows users to conduct document review, markup, and redaction; perform advanced searches and analytics; and monitor the status of an eDiscovery project. Another eDiscovery provider, iConect, provides a review tool called **Xera** (http://www.iconect.com/xera), but it supports access only through the Safari browser.

At the time of this writing, two companies offer companion iPad apps for document review. However, they aren't designed to provide you with access to all of your case documents, only a subset. The first is **Relativity Binders** (http://bit.ly/1n24IMJ) from kCura, the developers of the great document review platform Relativity. The free app gives quick and easy access to your documents and the ability to download a subset to plan for depositions or other case events. You won't be able to code the documents, just review them. But it's definitely a handy tool if you are using Relativity to host case records. If you are a user of @LegalDiscovery's CasePoint eDiscovery platform, you will want to download **@Legal CasePoint** (http://bit.ly/1vkIch9), which provides roughly the same functionality as Relativity Binders.

The good news is that you have a number of options for reviewing case documents and other court files on your iPad; the bad news is that most of the apps work best with a smaller number of documents, as eDiscovery vendors seem to be shying away from developing apps for reviewing larger volumes of documents. If you have a really big case with a high volume of documents, you might want to think about doing your initial review on a desktop or laptop and then moving a smaller subset of those records to the iPad for further review and ultimate presentation at trial.

Taking and Reviewing Depositions

With document discovery nearing a close in the *Davis v. ACME Industries* case, you and opposing counsel are preparing to schedule depositions and hear from the plaintiff, the defendant's corporate representative, medical providers, and expert witnesses. There are a couple of great options for both taking and reviewing depositions on the iPad.

As a trial lawyer, my preparation for any deposition invariably involved creating an outline of all the topics and individual questions I wanted to cover with the witness. You can, of course, create outlines in any of the office suite apps mentioned in Lesson 1. **Microsoft Word** or **Documents to Go** will do a fine job of developing a basic outline.

You can use either of my favorite note apps, **Evernote** (http://bit.ly/1zERHNu) or **Microsoft OneNote** (http://bit.ly/1xocEez), to develop an outline and take notes during the deposition itself. These are very powerful apps for managing notes and other information; they can handle your outlines and a lot more. But if you're looking for something basic, why not try a dedicated outlining app instead?

Like most types of apps for the iPad, you can run a search for "outliners" in the App Store and find a lot of options. Two outlining apps I like and recommend are Cloud Outliner and OmniOutliner. For a basic, solid outlining program, try **Cloud Outliner** (http://bit.ly/1rgsZzk). There are no frills to this app; just start typing on a line and press enter to go to the next line. Use the buttons at the bottom to increase or decrease the indentation level, or move the line of text up or down. When you're done, you can synchronize the outline to your Evernote account. There are no for-matting options—it's just you and the text. But that may be all you need.

For more power and customization, check out **OmniOutliner** (http://bit.ly/1ojtSRP). The Local Documents page will show you all of the different ways you can trick out your outline, with lots of fonts, text colors, and background colors. You can also add multiple columns to create a spreadsheet-like look if your outline needs a bit more structure. Topics that contain particular types of data can also be configured for the outline, and the available options are Rich Text, Numbers, Dates, Duration, Pop-Up List, and Checkbox. You can add titles, subtitles, headings, separators, and other style features. Outlines can be converted to one of five formats—OmniOutliner, OPML, Dynamic HTML, Simple HTML, or Plain Text—and exported via email to other iPad apps or to an Omni Sync or WebDav server (see Figure 2.4 for a sample outline).

Figure 2.4 Sample Outline in OmniOutliner

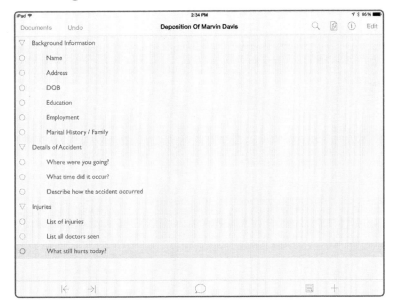

The best thing about these outlining apps is that you now have the ability to create deposition outlines easily and with a minimum of preparation, all on your iPad. No matter the type of deposition you are taking, you likely have a number of standard questions you ask each witness. With these apps, you can create and store these standard questions and easily insert them into your outline, along with any custom questions you may have for the witness.

If you are a user of the Liquid Lit Manager product, there's a Liquid Lit Manager (http://bit.ly/1ojvATj) app that provides access to your deposition outlines, along with all of your documents, in the same place.

You may prefer to use a pure note-taking app to take notes during a deposition. See Lesson 1 for the apps I recommend for taking handwritten or typed notes.

As time passes in your case, you attend and take the depositions of Marvin Davis, a corporate representative from ACME Industries; a couple of liability and damages experts; and some witnesses to the accident that gave rise to the lawsuit. Now it's time to review and annotate your deposition transcripts to prepare for mediation or trial. Not surprisingly, you'll find the iPad an ideal tool for this purpose. If you prefer to review depositions in PDF format, I've already mentioned a few great apps for viewing and annotating PDF files: **PDF Expert**, **iAnnotate PDF**, **PDFpen**, and **GoodReader** all do a great job of marking up PDF files.

If you want a tool with a bit more power and flexibility, then give **TranscriptPad** (http://bit.ly/1p2F1Xf) a look. The app allows you to create designations, flag important testimony, and even take notes in your deposition transcript for later reference. To get started, you'll first want to set up your case files. You can arrange the files either as a grid or with large folder icons (see Figure 2.5).

Figure 2.5 TranscriptPad Organizational Structure

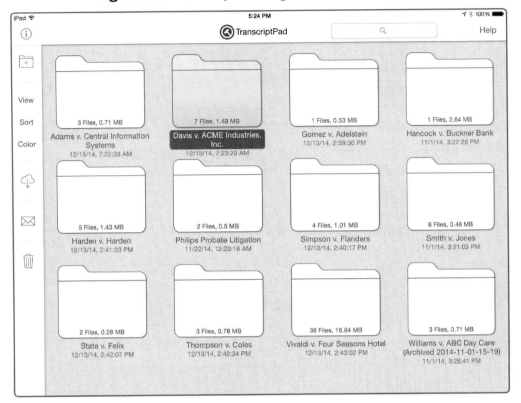

Now it's time to get deposition transcripts into the app. First, a caution: As of this writing, TranscriptPad accepts transcripts only in .txt format (and exhibits in PDF format). If you typically deal with depositions in .ptx format and want to use TranscriptPad, you will need to either (1) ask your court reporter to provide you with a .txt version of the transcript or (2) convert the .ptx file yourself by using West's free **E-Transcript Bundle Viewer** (http://tmsnrt.rs/1oDQiTf). Once you have all of your transcripts converted to .txt files, you'll find the choices for adding them to TranscriptPad all sound familiar:

- **Cloud Services.** Press the ***Cloud*** icon on the left and connect to your Box, Dropbox, Transporter, or WebDAV account. Then navigate to the folder with your deposition files and press ***Select Files or Folders*** at the bottom left of the dialog box. Select your files, or press ***Select All*** to choose everything in the folder. Press ***Import Selected Files and Folders***, and you'll see a list of your case folders. Press the correct case and the file is transferred.

- **Email.** Press on the transcript attachment in your email, tap ***Open In . . .*** , and then select ***TranscriptPad*** from the list.

- **iTunes.** Use the instructions above to transfer files directly from your computer to the iPad using iTunes.

When you use a cloud service or email to import files, you'll see a transcript verification screen, where you can edit the details of the deposition: the deponent name, volume number, and date. If you are importing exhibits, they will be filed automatically in a folder called ***Imported Exhibits*** within your case folder. You can also set up multiple folders inside a single case folder for the various depositions you may take in that legal matter.

When you're ready to review a deposition, just press on it in the case folder and you'll be taken to a reading view. To read the deposition hands-free, press the ***Auto-Scroll*** button at the bottom and adjust the dial to a comfortable reading speed. If you prefer, you can advance the deposition using the slider on the right by pressing the ***Page Up*** or ***Page Down*** buttons, or by simply flicking the page up or down with your finger.

Here's where the fun begins. As you review the deposition, you have the option to do a couple of things with the testimony, as shown in Figure 2.6:

- Assign an Issue Code. You can create unlimited issue code labels, but there are only six colors to set the labels apart.

- Highlight or underline text.

- Email testimony to yourself, your client, or others.
- Flag a section for later review and comment. You can also add text comments to Flags to keep notes for yourself or others.

To do any of these, just press the first and then last line of the testimony you want to highlight; the ***Annotate Designation*** box will appear, and you can assign any designation to the snippet that you like (see Figure 2.6).

Figure 2.6 Create Designations in TranscriptPad

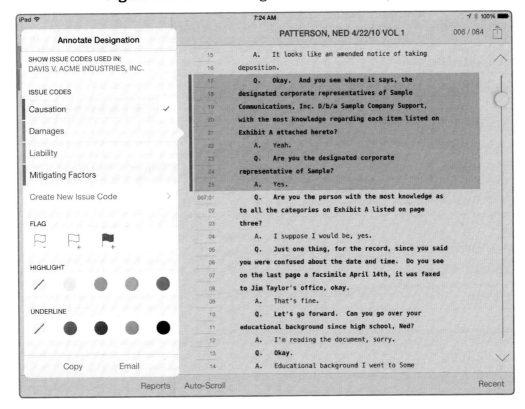

After you've finished highlighting and creating designations for your deposition (see Figure 2.7 for an example of an annotated deposition), you can of course keep it in your iPad for future reference and review. But to take advantage of TranscriptPad's real power, you'll want to check out the **Reports** function at the lower left. When you press that button, you'll see a number of different report types:

- PDF Reports—Detailed, Summary, or Full or Mini Annotated Reports (see Figure 2.8 for a sample report)

- Text Reports—Detailed or Summary

- Spreadsheet—to view the testimony in Excel

- Export to Trial Presentation Software—If you use **Sanction** or **TrialDirector** to present evidence at trial, this is an incredibly helpful option. TranscriptPad generates a file that you can import into either program for use in working with video depositions in the desktop versions of these programs. The option creates an Edit Decision List (EDL) that, when imported into either Sanction or TrialDirector, will automatically create clips for the edits you made, saving you hours of editing time.

Figure 2.7 Annotations in TranscriptPad

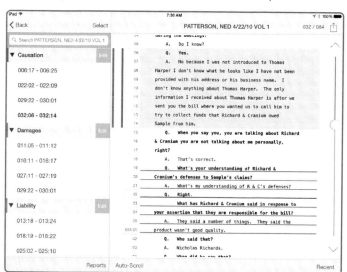

You can customize your reports by including as many or as few of your annotations as you like. You can include or exclude your Flags, Flag Notes, Highlights, Underlines, and Issue Codes. Once you finalize the settings for your report, press **Create Report**, and the report will appear in the panel to the right. When you press **Close**, you have the option of saving that report within TranscriptPad. To share the report with your client, the court reporter, or others, press the **Share** button at the upper right, which will give you the option to email it, print it, send it to one of the cloud services, or open it in another app.

Figure 2.8 Sample Detailed Report

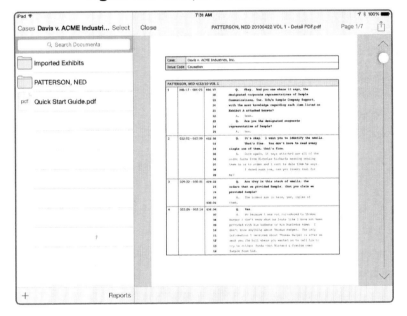

One of my favorite TranscriptPad features is the **Search** function. You can search through a single transcript or across all of the transcripts in a particular case file. Just use the search window at the top of the left menu to enter your search terms, press **Search** on the keyboard, and your results will appear. Select any result and the transcript will automatically scroll to the correct page and line where the term appears (see Figure 2.9).

Figure 2.9 Search in TranscriptPad

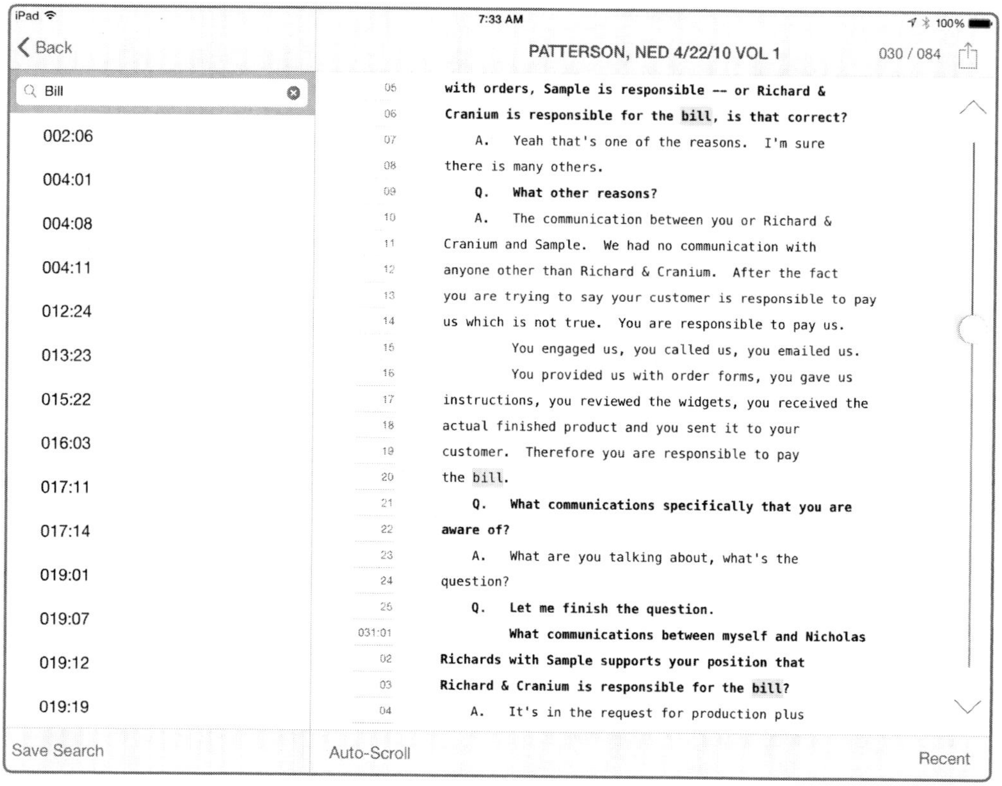

If for some reason you don't want to convert your .ptx files to text, or you prefer to keep transcripts in .ptx format, West has introduced the **Westlaw Case Notebook Portable E-Transcript** (http://bit.ly/1s0MtaH) app, which can only view depositions in .ptx format. You can receive depositions through the app via email, Dropbox, or iTunes. Once a file is loaded into the app, you can begin to review it. The annotation features in this app are not as advanced as those in TranscriptPad. Here you can only highlight and add notes to selected excerpts. To do that, press down on part of the desired testimony until the iPad's magnifying glass appears, and then lift up. You'll see options to ***Copy***, add a ***Note***, or ***Highlight***

the testimony. Before you select an option, make sure you move the blue buttons on the selected words until you have highlighted all of the testimony you want to designate. When you press ***Note***, a text box will appear into which you can type your note. If you press ***Highlight***, the text you selected will be highlighted. You can always see a list of your notes and highlights by pressing the open-book icon in the upper-right corner.

When you have finished taking notes and highlighting testimony, you can share the information by pressing the universal ***Share*** button in the upper-right corner. You'll see two options: to share ***With Notes*** or ***Without Notes***. With either option, the computer of the person who receives the deposition also must have a copy of the Westlaw Case Notebook; otherwise, the file won't open. Although this is a good option if you must work only with .ptx files, your options are somewhat limited if you want to use your annotations outside of the West ecosystem.

Another transcript review and annotation app is **Mobile Transcript** (http://bit.ly/1sUhi2S), a transcript subscription service. If your court reporter is a subscriber, you may not have to pay anything for your service. Just have the court reporter upload the Mobile Transcript to the site, and it will download to your iPad. If your court reporter does not use the service, you can purchase your own subscription and upload the transcripts yourself. In my opinion, however, the reviewing experience is not as professional as that of TranscriptPad or West's E-Transcript. You do not get to see page and line numbers, and you have to flip from page to page instead of smoothly scrolling through the transcript. While you can highlight text, search keywords, and send summaries in PDF, ASCII, Excel, or Sanction formats, you cannot create designations at the present time.

Many more deposition apps are available for the iPad, but these are the most noteworthy. A simple search for "depositions" in the iTunes App Store reveals dozens of apps offered by specific court reporting firms. Most of them appear to be based on a template, which provides access not only to transcripts but also to your account with the court reporter, deposition schedules, and even directions to a depo. Check to see if your court reporter offers access to your transcripts via the iPad.

One app that I really like takes a different approach to depositions: managing exhibits. **eDepoze**™ (http://bit.ly/1uVfaqj) is designed to store your exhibits and then share them with the witness and other lawyers at the deposition so they can view your exhibit in real time. You'll have to use the eDepoze web interface on your desktop to upload files and then fire up the app and see all of your exhibits, ready for the deposition.

The other attendees to your deposition can access eDepoze either on an iPad app or a browser-based web app. Users can open exhibits and annotate them, as well as save them to other apps. In Presentation Mode, you take control of the exhibit so that all users see what you want them to see: scroll to a specific page in a document, and all other users, as well as the witness, are taken to the same location on their apps (see Figure 2.10).

Figure 2.10 eDepoze

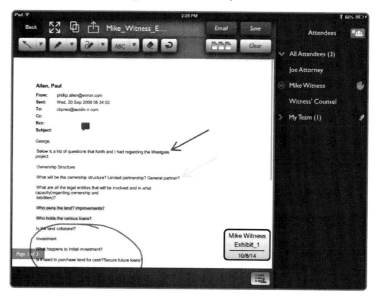

eDepoze also has a nice chat function so you can talk to others on your team. You can even share documents with others who are using the app—just drag a file over the name of the person with whom you want to share, and drop it. eDepoze is a great way to start eliminating paper exhibits from your depositions. The company is also a partner with kCura, so those of you using Relativity to review documents will be able to download files directly into the eDepoze app for use in depositions.

Finally, if real-time testimony is your thing, check out **iCVNet** (http://bit.ly/1xbrmCr), a free app for viewing real-time deposition transcripts. Court reporters using the Case CATalyst software can send real-time text over a wireless network, and attorneys can view, mark up, search, and email the transcript on their iPads.

You should now have reviewed all of the relevant case documents, and have taken all the deposition testimony you need to be prepared for trial. Before we head to the courthouse, let's make sure we have the right trial accessories.

Prepare for Trial with the Right Accessories

No matter whether you choose an iPad, laptop, or other technology for presenting evidence at trials, hearings, mediation, or other proceedings, you will always need to make sure you have the right equipment before you step into the courtroom. In the case of the iPad, that comes down to a fairly short list of items (assuming that most courts will offer a projector and screen):

- Keyboard
- Stylus
- Connection tools—adapters, network devices, and cables
- Printing apps

In this lesson, I'll provide a few recommendations for finding accessories in each of these areas, as well as some tips on constructing your iPad Trial Presentation toolkit.

Keyboards

If you plan on doing heavy-duty typing on the iPad during your trial or hearing, a keyboard is a must. The type of keyboard you use depends on your personal style—specifically, whether you prefer to have your keyboard separate from the iPad or connected to the device in an all-in-one case.

I prefer to keep my iPad as light and mobile as possible, and I also like a full-sized keyboard, so I am a big fan of the **Apple Wireless Keyboard** (https://www.apple.com/keyboard/). It is lightweight, very thin, and easy to stick into a computer bag. To connect it to your iPad, just turn the keyboard on, then go to *Settings > Bluetooth* on your iPad and press on *Apple Wireless Keyboard* to connect.

If you want an even lighter option, try the **Logitech Keys-to-Go Keyboard** (http://bit.ly/1GHu85E). It's just a quarter of an inch thick, so it easily slides into your computer bag. It's not a full-sized keyboard, but it is not too small to be uncomfortable. It's currently my favorite keyboard, because it is so light, thin, and easy to carry around.

Others prefer to create a more laptop-like experience with the iPad, and use a case with a built-in keyboard. There are many different keyboard cases on the market in several different styles, and my current favorite is the **Logitech Ultrathin Keyboard Cover** (http://bit.ly/1pEnHrR—iPad Air version). It really isn't a case at all; it's a keyboard with an aluminum backing and a slot you can use to prop up your iPad in either portrait or landscape mode. When you've finished working, just lay the face of the iPad down on top of the keyboard, and powerful magnets in the cover will connect to the iPad, creating a thin "case" for the tablet. For suggestions on and reviews of other cases, visit **iLounge** (www.ilounge.com).

If you expect to use the iPad frequently in court, you can't go wrong with any of these keyboards, because they all work with a wireless connection. If you are planning to show evidence from the iPad, either wirelessly or connected to the projector via a VGA cable, having the iPad connected to a keyboard in a case makes the device heavy and unwieldy. You might want to hand the iPad to a witness or carry it around the courtroom while you show exhibits, and a keyboard in a case would be too difficult to manage.

Stylus

If you prefer to type rather than handwrite notes on your iPad, then you can skip this section. But if using the iPad as a legal pad in court appeals to you, then you must have a stylus. I have tried many, and for me there are two common-sense criteria for a good stylus. First, it needs to write like a pen; there are too many styli out there that write like crayons, with big text and little control. Second, the stylus should feel like a pen. It should have a good heft and not feel weightless.

I currently recommend two styli. The first is the **Wacom Bamboo** (http://bit.ly/1suYk35). It has a good weight and the smallest point of any rubber-tipped stylus I have used (see Figure 3.1). I am not the best writer, but the Bamboo handles my writing well, and I can even read it.

For an even sharper point, try the **Adonit Jot Script** (http://bit.ly/1vHqMgJ). It uses Bluetooth to connect directly to the iPad, helping the app to understand the motions being made by the stylus. Its tip is very similar to a ballpoint pen, and it really feels like writing with one when you use it. (See Figure 3.2.)

Figure 3.1 Wacom Bamboo Stylus

Figure 3.2 Adonit Jot Script Stylus

There are dozens of other styli from which to choose, and many of them are reviewed at iLounge. By the time you read this, there will probably be many more new models, all trying to capture the perfect writing experience on the iPad.

Your Courtroom Toolkit

The tools you might use to display evidence on the iPad will depend, in part, on the venue where you are doing the presenting. Courtrooms and other meeting locations all have different equipment, and you may find that tools that work in one court will not work in another. For this reason, it's important to have a basic "toolkit" of connectors, so you are ready for every eventuality. Fortunately, the list is not long:

VGA adapter. For now, assume that the courtroom will at least have a projector and screen (if it doesn't, see **Projector and Screen**, below). The single best accessory you can buy for your iPad is the VGA adapter. If you have an iPad Air, Mini, or 4th-Generation iPad, you'll need a "Lightning to VGA" adapter (http://bit.ly/YlrgqU). For all older models, you'll need a "30 Pin to VGA" adapter (http://bit.ly/9rfAQW). They both connect your iPad to the projector's VGA port. The courtroom *should* have VGA cables, but if it doesn't, you may need some of your own. The VGA adapter is not long, so expect to be on a short leash if you use it with a projector, or be prepared with a VGA extension cord for greater mobility.

> *Note:* If you're using an older iPad (3rd Generation and earlier), you'll find that the 30-pin adapter easily disconnects from the iPad, so it can be an inconvenient tool to use (the Lightning adapter provides a fairly secure connection that will not easily come loose). Some presenters have reported success using professional gaffer tape to anchor the 30-pin adapter to the iPad. Still, the VGA adapter is what you will likely use most often until more courtrooms offer high-definition projection devices, or you decide to use a VGA-to-HDMI converter (see below).

Digital AV adapter. If the courtroom does have a projector with a high-definition (HDMI) port or a high-definition television, you can connect your iPad to it using Apple's Digital AV adapter (http://bit.ly/ydEsBX for the 30-pin model, http://bit.ly/UZQVp9 for the Lightning model). It works the same as the VGA adapter, but it's for high-definition devices. However, if you have access to high-definition projection capabilities, I recommend that you spring for the Apple TV instead.

Apple TV. The Apple TV (http://bit.ly/3ddZWM) is a wondrous device. Just plug it into the HDMI port of a projector or television, then connect it to the same network as your iPad, and you can wirelessly present from your iPad (see the sidebar below for specific instructions). The Apple TV gives presenters the freedom to move around the courtroom untethered, presenting evidence or showing other documents onscreen, or interacting with a witness during examination. Assuming you have the right equipment in the courtroom and you test your equipment ahead of time, the Apple TV provides a great trial presentation experience. I cannot stress enough the "test your equipment ahead of time" recommendation; due to screen-size reduction or degradation, your Apple TV may not display the way you want when you set it up. Make sure you get to the courtroom well in advance so you can set it up and fully test it out.

Other mirroring software. If you don't want to buy an Apple TV or the projector doesn't have an HDMI connection, there are several good software alternatives that can mirror your iPad through a laptop. My favorite is **AirServer** (www.airserver.com)—it's only $14.99 and installs on your laptop. On your iPad, bring up the Control Panel, select *AirPlay*, find your laptop and turn mirroring to *On*. The screen of your iPad will magically appear on your laptop screen. Just connect the laptop to a projector, and you are free to present with your iPad free of cables or wires. **Reflector** (http://bit.ly/10HfzBh) is another good mirroring alternative.

Extension cords. If you must use a VGA connection, you may find that the projector or VGA cord is too short or too far from counsel table or wherever you plan to use your iPad. You might consider bringing an extra VGA extension cord when you go to court; 10- to 20-foot cables are available online for quite reasonable prices. Keep in mind, however, that most extension cables are "male to male," which means that you may need a "female adapter" to connect to the original VGA cable. The other end of your extension cord will connect to the Apple VGA adapter, which has a female end.

HD video converter. If you really want to present wirelessly with your Apple TV but the projector is VGA-only and AirServer is not an option, you might consider an HD Video Converter. This is a tool that fits between the VGA cord and your Apple TV. It essentially takes the high-definition signal from the Apple TV and converts it to VGA format.

One of the more popular converters is the **Kanex ATV Pro** (http://bit. ly/1vJvE3Z); just plug your VGA cable into one end and the other into your Apple TV. **Note:** I was never able to get any converter to work well with my iPad—the output always looked more like a square, which makes the iPad screen look a bit squashed. But if you're interested in using an HD video converter and don't mind a slightly squashed display, the Kanex may be for you (see Figure 3.3).

Figure 3.3 Kanex ATV Pro

Speakers. If you plan to play depositions, videos, or audio recordings through your iPad, you'll want to pack some lightweight speakers for use in court. Rather than carry a lot of extra power and connection cords, though, think about using Bluetooth speakers. They have no wires, so you can place them anywhere in the room for maximum benefit. By going to Amazon and searching for "Bluetooth portable speakers," you'll find many good options. Recommended products include the **Jawbone JAMBOX Wireless Bluetooth Speaker** ($199, http://bit.ly/10Hi72h) and the **Logitech UE Mini Boom** ($115, http://amzn.to/1BNQotI).

Projector and screen. You may be in a courtroom without a screen or projector; make sure to call the court ahead of time to ask about the available technology so you have the right tools. You might choose to bring your own projector, one with an HDMI port, so you can run the Apple TV without any VGA issues. I won't be recommending any projectors here, so take some time to do your homework and find the right projector to suit your needs.

Power supply for your iPad. The normal battery life of an iPad is around ten hours, which should be enough to get you through a whole day of trial. If you are relying on the iPad as your sole trial presentation tool, however, don't take the chance that the battery will last all day. Throughout the day, make sure you plug the iPad into a charger whenever you aren't using it.

If you're in a location where using the iPad's charger is not convenient, consider buying a battery designed to recharge the iPad. Some of the best external batteries are made these days by **Anker** (http://bit.ly/1uuTP6R); you can't go wrong with any of the choices.

Printing from your iPad. Printing documents at the courthouse presents unique challenges. Lawyers who bring a laptop to trial can connect it to a portable printer to print out jury instructions, exhibits, or other documents. Printing from an iPad is more complicated because it cannot connect via cable to a printer. Dozens of printers are "AirPrint-Enabled"—that is, they connect wirelessly to your iPad so you can print without a wired connection—but as of this writing, none of those printers were portable.

Several apps allow you to print from your iPad. Two of my favorites are **Printer Pro** (http://bit.ly/1vKBMKl) and **Print n Share** (http://bit.ly/1s6zxAd). However, to use them you'll still need your laptop; these apps work by connecting to your desktop or laptop and sending a signal to the printer. If your goal in using an iPad at trial is to make your presentations lighter and less cluttered, bringing a laptop along to connect to a printer seems to defeat the purpose.

The **xPrintServer** (http://bit.ly/Pr3poq) by Lantronix is an interesting option for lawyers who want to print at trial. The small device eliminates the need to bring a laptop. Just connect the server box to a wireless router, which is also connected to your portable printer, and xPrintServer will auto-discover the printer—the setup is almost that simple. When you want to print a document from the iPad, just navigate to the **Print** command in the app you're using, and the name of the portable printer should appear in your list. Just a few taps and your document should print. The xPrintServer currently costs $99 for home use and $199 for the network version.

Now that you have all the equipment you need to display your iPad to a judge or jury, it's time to head to court.

A Step-by-Step Guide for Connecting Apple TV

1. Locate the HDMI outlet on the projector and plug in the HDMI cable from your Apple TV (see Step #1, Figure 3.4).

2. Plug the Apple TV into a power outlet. It will display a Welcome message on the screen (Step #2, Figure 3.4).

3. The Apple TV connects to your iPad through a wireless connection (Step #3, Figure 3.4). There are a couple of ways to connect:

   - Use a wireless router—buy a cheap dual-band router from Amazon or your local technology store. You don't need an Internet connection; you just need to create a network through which both devices can connect. Simply plug in the router, and the network should be visible to the Apple TV and iPad.

   - Use your own wireless card, such as a **MiFi**. This is a better option than using the courthouse wireless connection, but it can still be subject to poor reception depending on your location.

   - Use the courtroom's wireless connection, if available. This is only recommended as a last resort because courtroom connections are not always the most reliable.

4. To connect Apple TV to the network, navigate to ***Settings > General > Network > Wi-Fi***. Choose the right connection, and then enter the password for the network. If you are using a wireless router, change the default password that came with it (usually "admin") and set a password to make sure no one tries to access the network while you're in the courtroom.

   Connect the iPad to the same network. On the iPad, go to ***Settings > Wi-Fi***. Choose a network, and enter the password you created for the router Step #4, Figure 3.4).

5. To display your iPad on the projection screen, swipe up from the bottom of the iPad screen to bring up the Control Panel. Press ***Airplay***, then ***Apple TV***, and then set ***Mirroring*** to ***On*** (see Figure 3.5). You should now be able to see your iPad screen projected onto the projection screen.

Figure 3.4 Setting Up Apple TV with a Projector

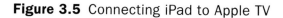

Figure 3.5 Connecting iPad to Apple TV

Legal Research

Back in the days when I was actively trying cases, I would sometimes haul an entire briefcase full of research to court every day during a trial: rules of civil procedure, rules of evidence, and copies of case law printed out and highlighted (with multiple copies for opposing counsel and the judge). If I were still trying cases today, one of my favorite things would be carrying all my legal research on my lightweight, slim iPad instead of lugging around all that paper.

Another advantage to having an iPad in the courtroom is that you can have your entire law library at your fingertips via online research services. Now, when opposing counsel cites a case that's new to you, you can look it up, read it, perhaps review related cases, and respond to their arguments immediately rather than saying, "Sorry, Judge, I'll have to review that case and get back to you."

In this lesson, we'll cover the best apps that allow you to conduct legal research on your iPad, whether you're in the courtroom or any other location.

Finding Case Law

One of the most important research apps you can install on your iPad is one that gives you anytime, anywhere access to case law. And as you might expect, the two big research services—Westlaw and Lexis—have you covered in that regard.

LexisAdvance (http://bit.ly/1r0Eycy) provides a great interface for researching LexisNexis databases. There's a "smart search" box at the top, which you'll use to enter all of your search terms, or even a citation. As you begin to type your terms, LexisAdvance tries to predict your query and give you suggested searches that contain the words you have keyed in. Below the search box are filters you can use before you even begin your search. You can search All Content Types or limit your search to a particular type of content. A jurisdictional filter lets you select All Jurisdictions, U.S. Federal, or a particular state. You can even filter your search by Practice Area, with listings ranging from Administrative Law to Workers' Compensation.

Let's say you represent ACME Industries, and the judge has entered a ruling against your client that you believe to be improper. Doing a quick search in Texas for "abuse of discretion," you'll notice that you have come up with a lot of cases—61,499. A list of those cases appears to the right; you can save that search to a folder, or sort it by Relevance, Document Title, Jurisdiction, Court, or Date (see Figure 4.1a).

The list of cases is really too long to review, so let's filter it. You seem to recall a couple of cases on abuse of discretion that came from the Texas Supreme Court within the past ten years, so you set the timeline to search for cases back to 2004 that were decided by the Texas Supreme Court.

You're down to 309 cases now, and you can further filter the results by Practice Area, Attorney, Law Firm, Keyword, or Judge. Once you are ready to read cases, you'll get an exact replica of what you would find if you were conducting research on Lexis from your office computer.

Just press on a hyperlink to be taken to a referring case or headnote, and press the ***Share*** button to save the case to a folder or email it to yourself or others (see Figure 4.1b).

Figure 4.1a LexisAdvance Search Results

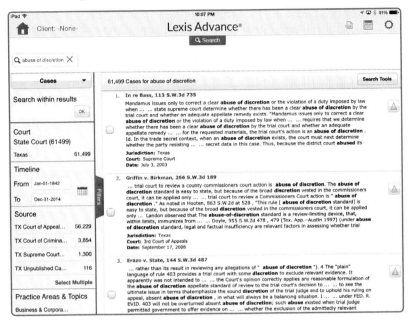

Figure 4.1b Saving or Sharing in LexisAdvance

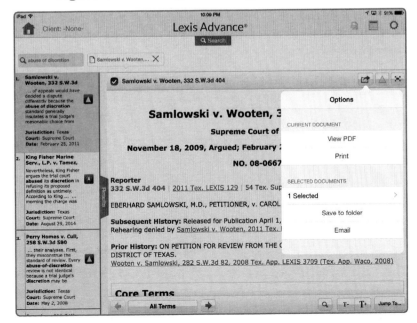

LexisAdvance is a great app, and if you're a subscriber to the service, using it on your iPad is a no-brainer.

West's answer to LexisAdvance is **WestlawNext** (http://bit.ly/ZqQJFp). Just like Lexis, you can run any search from the box at the top of the home screen, but you can also browse cases, key numbers, statutes, regulations, secondary sources, and more. My search for "abuse of discretion" returned only 10,000 results, and while I have a few more filtering options, I am unable to search by court (see Figure 4.2). When you select a case, you will have familiar options: you can email, print, save offline or to an online folder, or add a note. You can also create a KeyCite Alert to be notified when a new opinion cites the current result. The interface is not quite as slick as LexisAdvance, but if you're a West subscriber, you should definitely be using this app.

Figure 4.2 WestlawNext

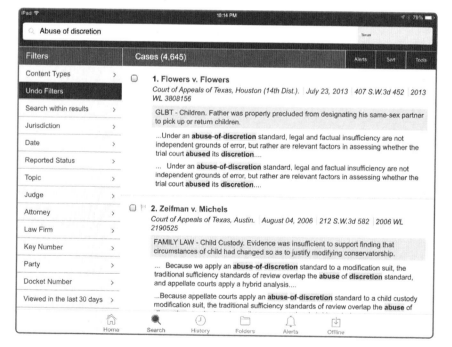

The last app I'll mention in this area was the first to the iPad, and for some is still the favorite. **Fastcase** (http://bit.ly/1tjSPls) is also free, but with it you can actually access many of Fastcase's features without having a paid subscription. Many of you reading this book may already get Fastcase for free, courtesy of your state bar; if so, you should definitely take advantage of this app. If you're not already a West or Lexis customer, I unreservedly recommend Fastcase for your iPad research, primarily because you can get so much done for free. I know several lawyers who do subscribe to Westlaw or Lexis but still use the Fastcase app first, to avoid incurring charges on a paid service.

From the bottom of Fastcase's main screen, you can conduct a New Search, find Recent searches, view Saved cases, and adjust your Settings. From the New Search page, you can search case law and search or browse statutes. To search for a case, press Search Case law, enter your search terms, and select filters—Jurisdiction, Date Range, and Authority Check—to narrow your search (see Figure 4.3a).

Figure 4.3a Fastcase Search

From the results screen, your ability to filter results is a bit more limited than in the West and Lexis products. You still have access to the full case law and an "Authority Check" that lists those cases citing an opinion either generally or within the opinion itself (see Figure 4.3b). You can also save a particular case by pressing on the ***Save*** button.

Figure 4.3b Fastcase Search Results

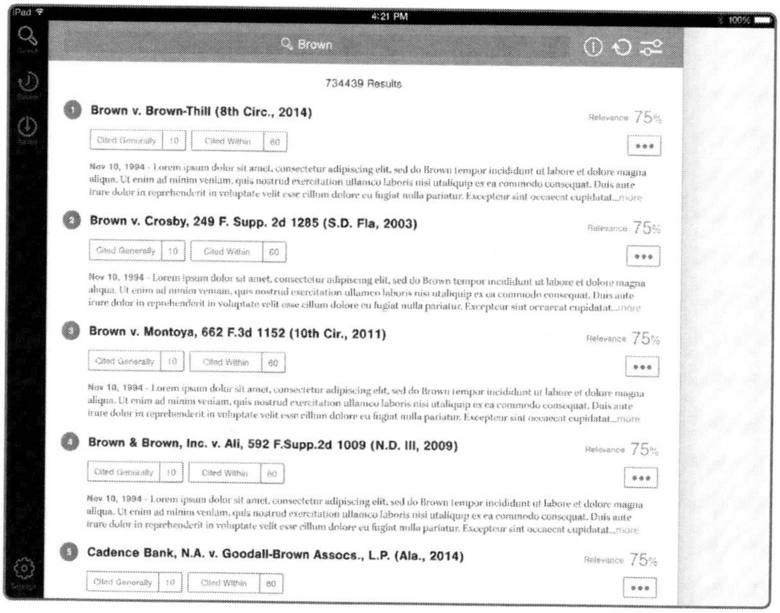

If you upgrade to the premium edition of Fastcase, you get a number of additional useful features, including:

- Unlimited customer support
- Dual-column printing of opinions
- More powerful sorting tools
- The ability to email an opinion or your search results
- Visual maps of search results

- Access to more libraries, such as court rules, administrative regulations, and constitutions
- Newspaper search, people finder, business intelligence, and forms
- Unified search within PACER

As of this writing, the cost for a Fastcase subscription ranges between $65 and $95 per month, depending on the plan. But the free version is definitely worth the download, especially if you don't have access to other online research services.

Rules and Statutes

Whenever you're in court for trial or a hearing, you will occasionally need access to rules or statutes—rules of civil procedure, rules of evidence, or statutes that may be specific to your case. Very rarely will you find all of this information in one printed volume, and when you do, it's usually a thick, heavy publication. Let's take a look at some iPad apps that will allow you to leave those rule and code books back at the office.

FYI. Not all states have made their rules or statutes available on the iPad. The apps I list below currently provide coverage for only a small number of states. In writing this book, I searched through the App Store for rules for all states, and I have listed in *Beyond the Lessons* what was available at the time of publication. If you don't see your state listed below, head to the App Store on your iPad and do a search for "**[state] law,**" "**[state] rules,**" or something similar.

And a **word of caution:** Remember at the beginning, when I mentioned that some developers haven't updated their apps in a long time? Well, that applies to the rules and statutes apps as well. Some of the apps you might find in the App Store have not been updated in some time— which means that the rules and statutes haven't been updated either. If you choose to use one of these apps, *please* make sure you check the currency of the legal sources you access.

Currently, my favorite rules/statute app is simply called **Rulebook**™ (http://bit.ly/1tgxNXf). It offers access to court rules and selected statutes of 21 states, all of which are available on an à la carte basis. You can also download style manuals such as the *Bluebook* or the *ABA Model Rules of Professional Conduct*. Prices run from $2.99 up to $24.99 depending on the title. Rulebook provides some basic formatting and annotation options. You can highlight relevant or important text, bookmark rules or statutes, add your own notes to them, or email them to others (see Figure 4.4).

Figure 4.4 Rulebook

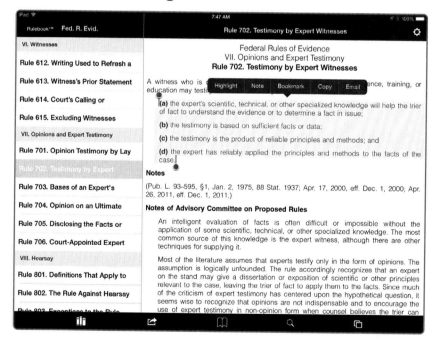

For a while, my favorite app for rules and statutes was **LawBox** (http://bit.ly/1zCU6YV). Unfortunately, since I wrote the first edition, the app is now only offered to certain organizations. If you're a Texas lawyer, you're in luck, because the app developer offers a version called **Texas Bar Legal** (http://bit.ly/1EBafyW), with access to all Texas codes and rules, as well as the Federal Rules of Evidence, Civil Procedure, and Appellate Procedure. Although the app is free to download, to use it you'll need to become a member of the State Bar of Texas's Computer and Technology Section—but I think it's worth $25 a year to have mobile access to all Texas statutes and rules. To join, visit http://www.sbot.org.

Another great feature of Texas Bar Legal (and another reason I'm sad the app isn't available to more lawyers) is an Annotations tool that provides access to case law within the app (see Figure 4.5). Just select a rule or statute and press the **Annotations** button, and you'll be given a list (not exhaustive, but decent) of Google Scholar (http://scholar.google.com) search results citing the rule you specified.

Figure 4.5 Texas Legal

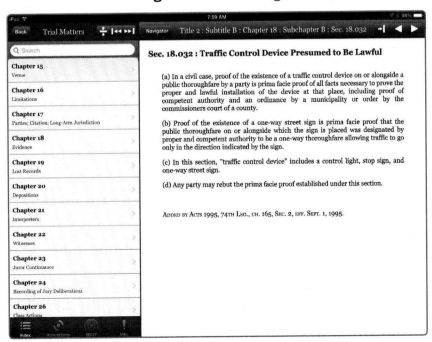

If you happen to live in a state where Thomson Reuters (West) publishes your rulebooks, you might want to take advantage of **ProView** (http://bit.ly/1vVuumY). The app is free, but you must purchase the paper publication or ebook in order to access it on your iPad. At this writing, ProView offers access for rule and code books for almost every state, with more than 300 federal and national titles (see Figure 4.6).

The bound rulebooks can get a little pricey—most of the books are $100 or more—but you do get quite a bit more for your buck than with either Rulebook or Texas Legal. You'll have access to rule amendments, the ability to transfer your highlights/notes/bookmarks to updated versions, and a direct link to WestlawNext or other Thomson Reuters platforms to conduct further research.

Figure 4.6 ProView

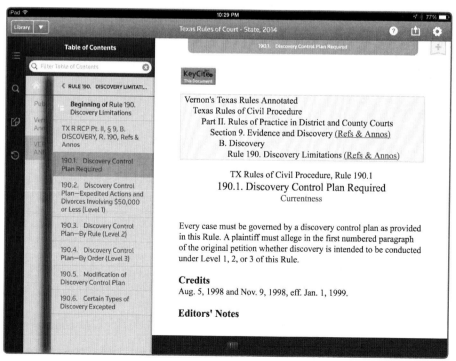

Federal Court Research

There's one last must-have type of app to mention in this lesson for those of you who practice regularly in federal court. The ability to access your PACER account while out of the office can be really convenient, and there are a couple of apps that can make that a snap. My favorite is **FedCtRecords** (http://bit.ly/115wsWs), which provides full access to civil court records within PACER. The app was designed for the iPhone, but it works just fine when expanded to double size on the iPad. With FedCtRecords you can view Attorney Information (you can even download contact information to your device), Case Summary, Deadlines/Hearings, Docket Report, and Party Information (see Figure 4.7a).

Figure 4.7a FedCtRecords

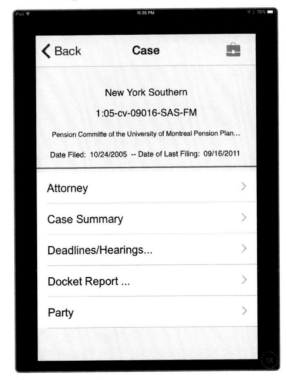

Even better, you also have access to any document filed in any case, assuming it's publicly available within PACER. You can view the document, email it to yourself or others, or open it up in another app (such as GoodReader, PDF Expert, or TrialPad) (see Figure 4.7b).

Figure 4.7b Access to Documents in FedCtRecords

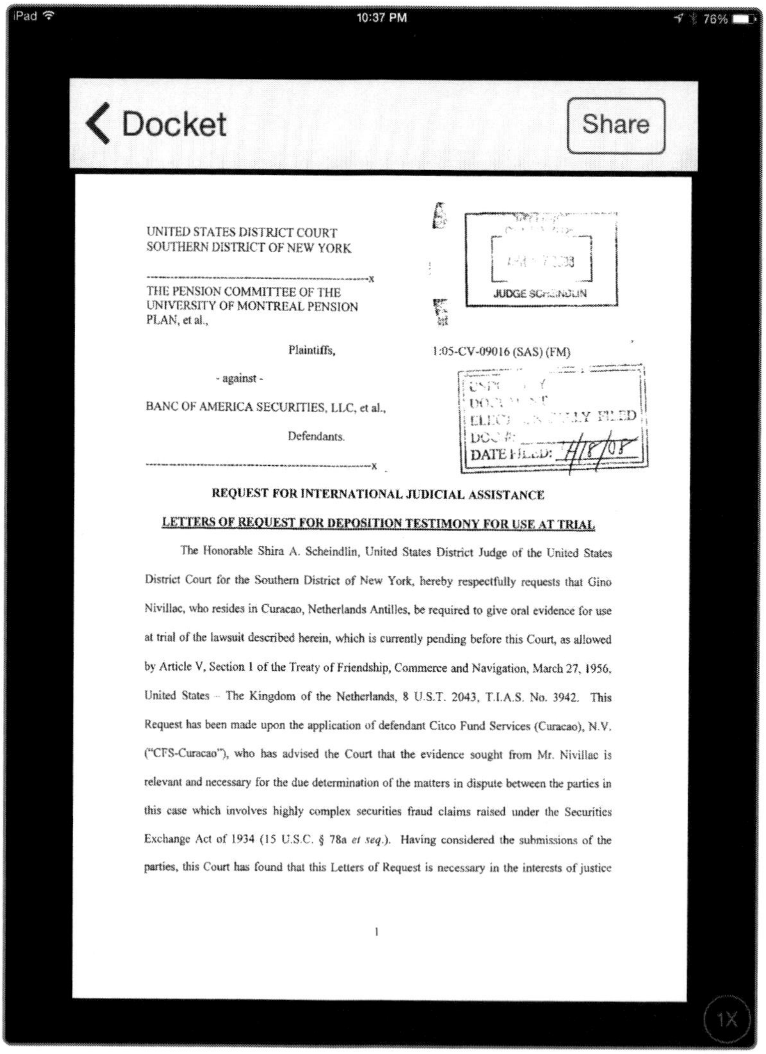

UNITED STATES DISTRICT COURT
SOUTHERN DISTRICT OF NEW YORK

THE PENSION COMMITTEE OF THE UNIVERSITY OF MONTREAL PENSION PLAN, et al.,

Plaintiffs,

- against -

BANC OF AMERICA SECURITIES, LLC, et al.,

Defendants.

1:05-CV-09016 (SAS) (FM)

REQUEST FOR INTERNATIONAL JUDICIAL ASSISTANCE

LETTERS OF REQUEST FOR DEPOSITION TESTIMONY FOR USE AT TRIAL

The Honorable Shira A. Scheindlin, United States District Judge of the United States District Court for the Southern District of New York, hereby respectfully requests that Gino Nivillac, who resides in Curacao, Netherlands Antilles, be required to give oral evidence for use at trial of the lawsuit described herein, which is currently pending before this Court, as allowed by Article V, Section 1 of the Treaty of Friendship, Commerce and Navigation, March 27, 1956, United States – The Kingdom of the Netherlands, 8 U.S.T. 2043, T.I.A.S. No. 3942. This Request has been made upon the application of defendant Citco Fund Services (Curacao), N.V. ("CFS-Curacao"), who has advised the Court that the evidence sought from Mr. Nivillac is relevant and necessary for the due determination of the matters in dispute between the parties in this case which involves highly complex securities fraud claims raised under the Securities Exchange Act of 1934 (15 U.S.C. § 78a *et seq.*). Having considered the submissions of the parties, this Court has found that this Letters of Request is necessary in the interests of justice

1

FedCtRecords is an example of an app that is still usable despite a relative lack of updates over the years. While its developer has provided bug fixes or other small updates since its initial release in 2011, the design and functionality remain the same. And that's okay. It provides you with everything you need to effectively access your PACER account.

A newer app for accessing PACER is **DkT** (http://bit.ly/1uVd0Hk). The app is much more modern than FedCtRecords and reasonably well designed. However, it only provides the docket for a particular case; unlike FedCtRecords, you cannot access attorney and party information or case deadlines. But if access to the docket and associated filings is all you need, then DkT does a fairly good job. You can view filings within the app and email them to yourself or others. If you want to save the document to your iPad, however, you are currently limited to a few apps; on my iPad I was limited to OneNote, Evernote, and Basecamp.

Remember, there are dozens, if not hundreds, of legal research apps available for the iPad, covering both state and federal courts. The apps mentioned in this chapter cover the basics: general legal research, rules and statutes, and federal court records. Take the time to research these apps yourself to decide which one makes the most sense for the way you want to access these resources when you are out of the office.

You now have access to all the case law and statutory support you'll need to make your case in *Davis v. ACME Industries*, which is now scheduled for trial. Let's get ready to pick a jury.

Lesson 5

Picking a Jury, iPad Style

As a technology-focused person, the most frustrating part of a trial for me has always been jury selection. While trying cases, I was usually relegated to sketching out a grid on a legal pad because no good technology was available for keeping track of my voir dire activities. Fast forward to the present, and the iPad is here with a solution to my frustration—or make that solutions—in the form of several innovative jury selection apps. These apps make it relatively easy to keep all the information about your jury in one place, where you can review or share it with others.

Before diving in, however, a word of caution: these apps require quite a bit of data input before they can be used most effectively. For best results, you should already have all the information on each potential juror entered before you even start the jury selection process. In many courts, however, you might not see the jury list until 15 minutes before voir dire begins. In most cases, these apps work best for those trials where you receive the jury list at least a few hours ahead of time, if not a whole day.

One of the better apps for picking a jury is **iJuror** (http://bit.ly/1CflPfn). When you open the app for the first time, you'll see several options—New Trial, Saved Trials, Browse All Jurors, Charts & Stats, and Link to Dropbox or Box (see Figure 5.1a).

Figure 5.1a iJuror Main Screen

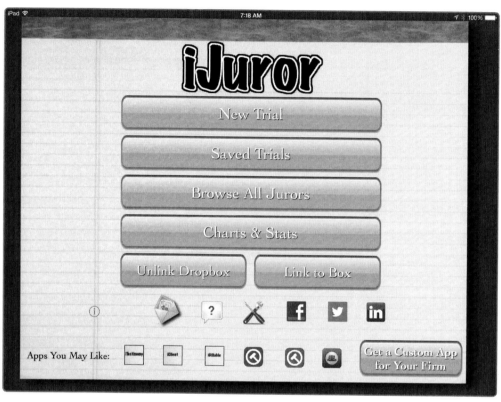

Select **New Trial**, and on the next screen enter the trial name and the size of your jury, plus alternates. On the next screen, you'll see blank rows of chairs, where you will seat your jury panel. To match the screen to the seating arrangement in the courtroom or jury room, select **Seat Layout** in the upper-right corner and select the number of rows and number of seats per row. Your main screen should now match the voir dire panel seated in front of you.

Here's where the work comes in. Press on an empty seat and a juror information screen will appear. You can enter the name, juror number, employment, hometown, and any notes you have on the main screen. Across the middle of the screen is a set of buttons that will take you to various social media sites and search engines, where you can learn more information about the potential juror if you like. When you press ***Enter/View Basic Juror Details*** at the top of the screen, you can select other demographic information—age, sex, race, marital status, children, education, and your current opinion of the person (you can also create custom spinner fields to capture any information you want under the ***Settings*** menu). Press ***Done*** on that screen, and the ***Save Information***, and on the main screen you'll see that seat is now filled with a juror. *Tip:* If you press the ***gear*** button in the upper-right corner, you'll find options to "quick enter" basic juror information, edit multiple jurors at once, enter custom juror questions, and much more. Once you've finished entering all your juror information, you should have a full panel on the main screen (see Figure 5.1b).

Figure 5.1b Seating a Jury with iJuror

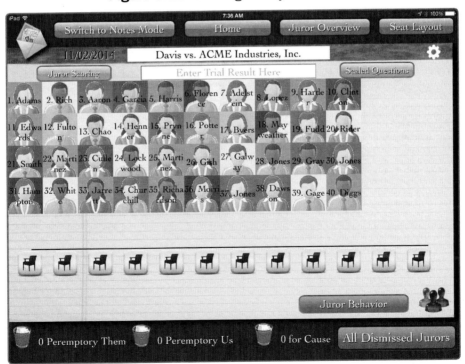

Once you start jury selection, just press on a juror to take notes on his or her responses. If you added custom questions, you can also add the answers here as well, and score each juror based on his or her response. To view your entire panel at a glance, press ***Juror Overview***, and you'll see a digital version of the legal pad I once used at trial (see Figure 5.1c).

Figure 5.1c Juror Overview in iJuror

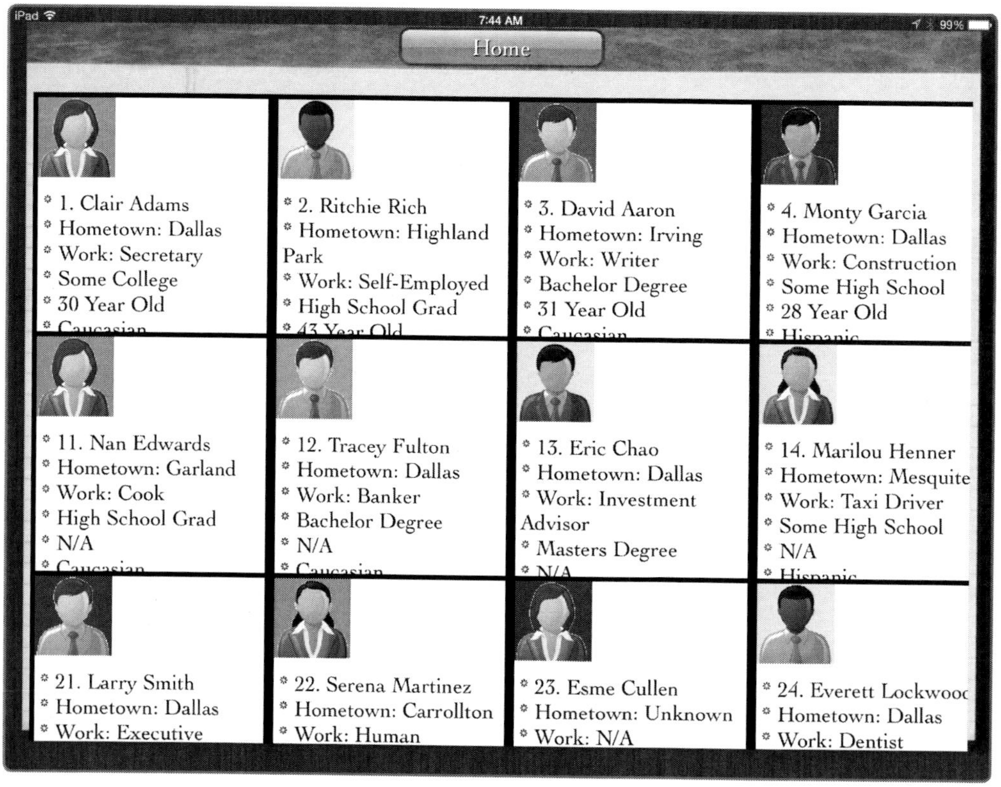

You can also share this information with others on your trial team via either Bluetooth or File Sharing through Dropbox, Box, or iTunes. However, the person you're sharing with must also be using iJuror to receive the file. Once you've finished with jury selection, simply drag the panelists into the appropriate location—the Peremptory "wastebaskets" (for Us or Them), the For Cause wastebasket, or into a seat on the final jury panel.

If you use iJuror, you might also want to try **iJuror Stickies** (http://bit. ly/ZXoaQg), which enables you to keep additional information on jurors. You can create rows with different colors and group multiple jurors into several categories. Like iJuror, you can also share anything created here with others via email or printing. My only gripe is that this functionality should have been built into iJuror, where all information could exist in the same place. It's a great idea for an app, but it belongs with the other iJuror information.

Your iJuror information is also available online through **iJuror Connect** (https://www.ijurorconnect.com), a subscription service that allows you to enter all your jury information on a desktop or laptop and then import the data into the iPad app. When you've finished with your case, you can import the updated information back into the online database to keep a permanent record of all your jury trials. It would certainly be more convenient if the app and online service could communicate and sync directly with each other; hopefully, this feature will be added in future releases. Pricing runs between $30 and $140 per month, depending on the size of your firm.

JuryStar (http://bit.ly/1qY0aSw) offers a different spin on jury selection—ranking jurors based on their answers to your voir dire questions. Like iJuror, you'll have to do quite a bit of data entry on your jury pool. To get started, press the *Trials* button at the bottom, then the **+ *sign*** next to Saved Trials. Enter the name of your trial, then specify the size of your jury pool; JuryStar can display a pool of up to 3,025 panelists—55 rows of 55 jurors.

When you have created your trial, press the ***Enter Cells*** button at the bottom. Press on a jury seat, then on ***Juror Info***, and you will see a screen where you can enter basic information on the panelist: name, race, gender, age, marital status, education, and places for more demographic information and notes. This where the hard work is done. When you've finished entering information on each juror, tap the name to seat the juror in the grid above.

When the panel is completed, you can load your voir dire questions. Press **Load Questions** and then **+ sign** to add a new topic. You can then add as many questions under that topic as you like. The app comes pre-loaded with topics like Prior Jury Experience, Prior Legal Experience, and Experience with Law Enforcement, but you can create any topic you want. When you're ready to select the jury, press on the **Voir Dire** tab; all of the panelists you entered will be listed here, along with all of your questions at the bottom of the screen. As you go through your questions, press the panelist answering your questions, and then move the rating scale (currently with a range of −5 to +5) to indicate your opinion of how they answered your questions. Press the **Rate** button to assign the rating. You can also press **Like** or **Dislike** to indicate an overall opinion of the panelist (see Figure 5.2). After the questioning is completed, you can move to the **Strike Jurors** screen to indicate the jurors that are struck, either by you, the opposing party, or the court.

JuryStar offers no way to rank the jurors based on the scores you gave them—it simply provides the individual scores for each juror in that panelist's individual data cell. There's also no way to export your jury information to other formats outside of your iPad. **(Note:** As of the date of this edition, JuryStar had not been updated since 2012. The app still functions as described above.)

iJury (http://bit.ly/ZBL135) is similar to JuryStar in that it also allows you to score jurors on their answers to prepopulated as well as custom questions. When you set up a case, you are able to specify the number of panelists and whether you'll want to see civil, criminal, custom, or common voir dire questions. If you have your own custom questions, enter them on the setup page. Once your jury information is entered, you are able to see basic demographics for the panelists (as in iJuror). And when you select ***Group Score***, the questions you selected appear on that screen. As you question jurors, you can score their answers to your questions by pressing the + or − buttons (see Figure 5.2).

Figure 5.2 iJury

Like JuryStar, the app doesn't rank the jurors for you based on their scores—it merely provides a breakdown of the positive, negative, and neutral reactions you receive from them. The ability to export information is also limited. When you press the ***Export*** button, the basic case information, names of jury panelists, and demographic information are exported.

One last jury selection app is **JuryPad** (http://bit.ly/1tae75H), which has most of the same tools as the other apps but with a nicer user interface. In addition to the basic data entry fields (race, marital/education status, employer, etc.), there are other fields for military experience, civil or criminal trial experience, knowledge of the case or parties, and information on the panelist's family members. You can view the potential jurors as a list or in a seating chart, and add notes or other information from either view. You can also create custom voir dire templates. There is also no current method for ranking jurors or assigning them stars, but you can share the list of jurors via spreadsheet or text file, or with other JuryPad users.

If you have a paralegal or assistant who is able to observe the jury and a full-time jury consultant is out of your budget range, you might want to check out **JuryTracker** (http://bit.ly/1C11NJN). It's designed to record the reactions of your jury once they are seated (see Figure 5.3a). Just enter

Figure 5.3a JuryTracker

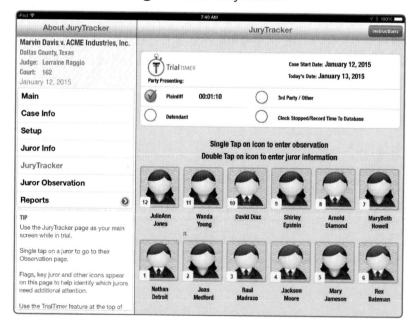

your basic case information and the names of your jurors. When you're ready to start, press the timer for the side that's asking the questions.

As jurors begin to react to the testimony, press on a specific juror to enter that reaction. You have a number of choices. You can note whether a juror is laughing, smiling, neutral, frowning, crying, angry, nodding or shaking his or her head, taking notes, being attentive, making eye contact, watching the time, fidgeting, daydreaming, or even sleeping (see Figure 5.3b). You can predict whether jurors will side with the plaintiff or defendant, characterize them as leaders or followers, and indicate whether the individual is a key juror. All of these observations will be stored, and you can later package them into reports by juror, the party presenting, a specific reaction, or a full chronological report. You can save these reports as text files, spreadsheets, PDFs, or in an email.

Figure 5.3b Observations in JuryTracker

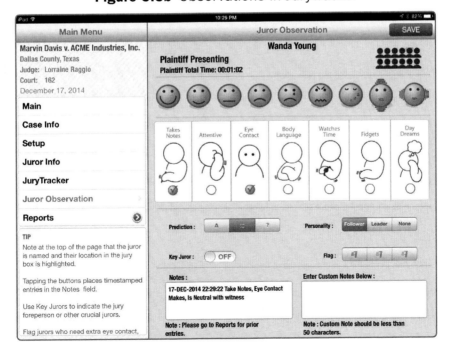

I think JuryTracker is a fun, interesting app for lawyers (or their assistants) who have a lot of time to do this during a trial.

As you can see, jury selection apps can be very interesting and useful, but only if you have the time to enter all the relevant information. If not, you may find that a legal pad is still your best friend during voir dire.

Now that your jury is seated, it's time to get down to the business of conducting a trial. The court is calling the case of *Marvin Davis v. ACME Industries, Inc.*

Evidence Presentation

Traditionally, lawyers have rarely presented their own digital evidence at trial. Paper is easy to present—just take the paper exhibit, hand it to the witness, or place it on a document camera for display to the jury. Digital presentation of exhibits or deposition testimony is more challenging.

During the time I served as a trial technologist for my law firm, I would never have recommended that a lawyer use technology alone at trial. My typical setup included a laptop with trial presentation software, extra monitors for the lawyers, and all sorts of cabling between my computer, the monitors, and the projector. Lawyers who must pay attention to the testimony and other trial activity would find it very difficult to also manage these multiple layers of technology.

The iPad has changed all that. Now, many lawyers are finding it downright easy to go to court and conduct a trial or hearing with only their tablets. At the heart of this revolution in evidence presentation are a series of apps that you can set up and use without the help of a trial technologist (of course, a technologist can help you out with this too, if you like). In this lesson, we'll take a look at trial presentation applications currently available for the iPad, as well as some others that can help you make your case to a judge or jury.

Evidence Presentation Apps

For years, the two giants of trial presentation technology have been TrialDirector and Sanction. They are both excellent evidence presentation applications, with very powerful capabilities for displaying exhibits as well as video deposition testimony synchronized with the transcript.

TrialDirector was late to the iPad app party, and did not roll out its TrialDirector for iPad app until 2012—long after several other developers had rushed to fill the void left by the two major evidence presentation providers in the iPad market. As of the date of this publication, Sanction still has no iPad companion app.

In my opinion, the best evidence presentation app for the iPad is currently **TrialPad** (http://bit.ly/1BOrw5o). It is the most full-featured app in its class. Getting started with TrialPad is simple—just press the **+** **_button_** at the upper left to name and create a New Case. You can then start adding documents to the case folder (see Figure 6.1a) using

Figure 6.1a TrialPad

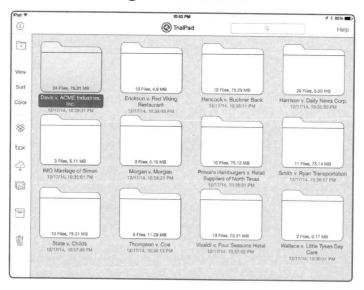

Dropbox, Box, a WebDAV server, or pulling pictures directly from the photos on your iPad. You can also transfer files via email or iTunes, or from any other app using the ***Open In . . .*** function.

TrialPad supports just about any document format you want to use, but I recommend that you convert most documents to PDF, because a PDF keeps the original formatting and is just easier to use on an iPad. You probably do not need to convert image files (JPEG, TIFF, PNG, etc.), because they will work just fine. TrialPad also supports any audio or video format supported by the iPad, which includes .wav, .mp3, .m4v, .mp4, .mov, and .avi files.

Once you have loaded your files into a case folder, you can begin to organize them. TrialPad allows you to create as many folders as you like, and it separates Documents from Multimedia—videos, audio, and the like. You also have the ability to assign exhibit numbers and stickers to documents and customize your folders with colors or special icons. In each folder you can sort exhibits by Name, Exhibit #, whether they are Admitted, or using custom criteria. Inside the folders you can do a lot of things with your exhibits—sort, reorder, duplicate, move, or delete them.

By the time you get into the courtroom, you'll have all your case files loaded and organized, and you'll also have your iPad connected to a pro-jector, high-definition television, or Apple TV (as explained in Lesson 3). When you first start TrialPad, the screen will only show black, because you don't want your jury to see any evidence until you're ready to show it to them. Along the bottom of the screen you'll see an ***Output*** button, which should be in the OFF position; slide it to ON and you'll see a couple of options:

- **Blank** shows a blank screen until you are ready to present evidence.
- **Freeze** shows a frozen version of the last exhibit you showed to the jury, while you prepare to show the next exhibit behind the scenes.

- **Present** is the button you press when you are ready to show an exhibit to the judge or jury.
- **Side by Side** will display two exhibits next to each other so the documents or images can be compared.

When you touch ***Present***, the jury does not see your "War Room" of folders, exhibits, and other things you might be doing on your iPad; all they see is the document you are presenting to them. When you display an exhibit, you have several annotation options along the top (see Figure 6.1b):

Figure 6.1b TrialPad Annotation Options

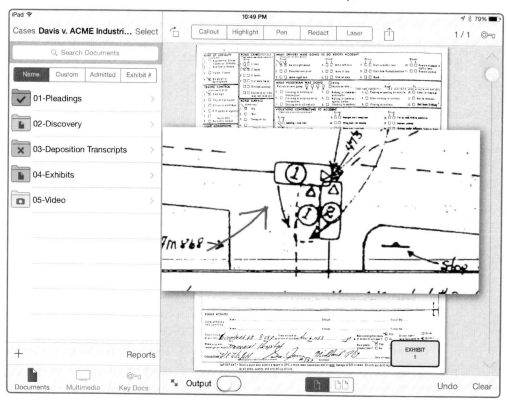

- **Callout**—With this button pressed, just drag your finger over the portion of the exhibit that you want to expand, and it will cut out and magnify that part of the document. You can have multiple callouts of one page, or even from two pages displayed side by side.

- **Highlight**—You can highlight relevant parts of an exhibit (press and hold for multiple colors).

- **Pen**—Use this option to draw or write on the exhibit (press and hold for multiple colors/thicknesses).

- **Redact**—Drag your finger around an area of the exhibit to hide it from the jury. This feature is useful if the judge rules a part of your exhibit inadmissible.

- **Laser**—Use this option to point out specific parts of an exhibit.

To the right of the annotation toolbar is the ***Key Documents*** button. As you present evidence, press this button to save pages or entire documents that are particularly important to the case. Then, press the ***Key Docs*** button in the lower left, and you'll have a complete listing of all the documents you tagged throughout the trial. This is an exceptionally helpful feature if you want to be able to go through the most important exhibits with a particular witness or during closing argument.

Press the **+** *sign* inside the Key Docs area, and you can create a **Whiteboard**, which allows you or a witness to use the pen to draw diagrams, calculations, or anything else you want to show a jury.

TrialPad can also show videos, including depositions, accident scenes, or other videographic evidence (see Figure 6.1c). You upload the videos the same way you upload other files, and they will be available to you in the Multimedia area. As you play the video, the controls stay up on your screen, so you can pause or stop the video at a moment's notice; these controls are not visible to the jury. You can take a snapshot of a video clip, which will be saved as a PDF file in your Documents area. You can also create a clip of a video within TrialPad. Just press the **Clip Video** button, and a separate dialog box will appear where you can select a smaller portion of the video for editing. If you press and hold on the edit bar, it will expand to allow for more precise edits. The capabilities here are pretty basic, so if you need more advanced video editing, you will need to use an application specifically designed for working with video.

Figure 6.1c TrialPad Multimedia Screen

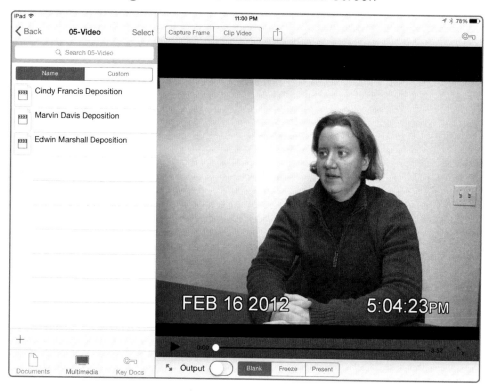

While TrialPad will show a video deposition, it does not currently have the capability to display a deposition that is synchronized with the transcript, like TrialDirector or Sanction (for that feature, see TrialDirector for iPad, below). To show depositions with accompanying scrolling testimony, you will need to create the file outside of TrialPad. Most videographers have access to software that can synchronize transcript to video for an additional fee. Alternatively, tools like **Camtasia** (www.techsmith.com/camtasia.html) will allow you to import the video and then add the transcript text as a caption; the video and synchronized text can then be viewed using TrialPad.

The best iPad apps allow you to share information outside the app, and TrialPad does not disappoint in this regard. Using the ***Share*** button (see Figure 6.1d), you can share a page or document by email; send it to Dropbox, Box, or a WebDAV server; or print it on a compatible printer.

Figure 6.1d Sharing in TrialPad

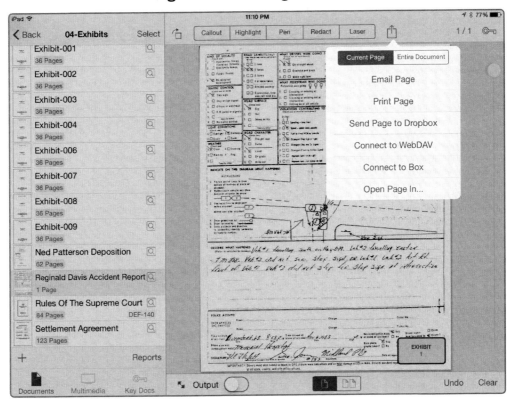

You can also create an Evidence Report, which will compile a listing of all your exhibits—documents, multimedia, and key documents; add exhibit numbers and other information; and save it all in a PDF file that can be emailed or printed. Even better, you can create an entire archive of your case to save off your iPad or share it with other TrialPad users. To do this, go back to the Cases screen and click the **File Box** button at the bottom left. Select the case(s) you want to archive, press **Backup**, and a complete copy of the entire case, with annotations and everything, will be created. To move it off your iPad, connect to iTunes, then use the File Sharing steps I explained in Lesson 2.

This is just a brief introduction to all that TrialPad can do. To learn more, visit the Support page on the Lit Software website (www.litsoftware.com).

For some, TrialPad's price may seem to be a dealbreaker. At $89.99, it is one of the higher-priced evidence presentation apps available. However, when compared to the $500 to $600 license fees for the desktop versions of TrialDirector or Sanction, it certainly seems like a good bargain.

ExhibitView (http://bit.ly/1nLriZS) comes the closest to TrialPad in terms of features—it has nearly the same annotation tools, and it offers better pen and line-drawing options. In fact, the two apps have very similar layouts (see Figure 6.2). But ExhibitView does not feel as polished as TrialPad; it doesn't offer the same functionality when working with videos, and there are no options for exporting documents for use by others. Given that both apps cost the same—$89.99—my opinion is that TrialPad is the better buy.

One of ExhibitView's strengths is that it is a companion app to a desktop software application of the same name. This means that you can create your case file within ExhibitView on your desktop or laptop and then transfer it to the iPad for use at trial. If you want to keep all the case files on your

Figure 6.2 ExhibitView

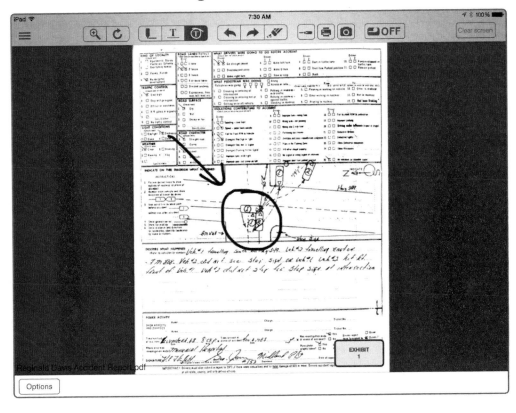

laptop, you can instead use the iPad as a remote control. Just connect your laptop to the projector, then connect your iPad to the laptop using a remote access tool like **SplashTop Remote Desktop** (http://bit.ly/ZW6YtE). Then you can operate ExhibitView from your iPad while leaving the laptop back at counsel table.

As mentioned above, **TrialDirector for iPad** (http://bit.ly/ZW8xb1) is the free iPad companion to the company's desktop application, which is arguably the best trial presentation software available. Having an iPad companion app presents a number of opportunities to firms that are already using this software. Now, trial technologists, either in-house or hired, who work with firms are able to use an iPad in the courtroom when assisting lawyers with trial presentation. Even better, however, these same trial technologists can now hand those lawyers the iPad and tell them, "You can do this yourself." The case can be created using the desktop software and then transferred to the iPad app, which can be used by any lawyer with only a little bit of training and practice. For those cases where evidence decisions must be made on the fly—for example, exhibits added or new deposition excerpts created—you will still want the full version of TrialDirector available in the courtroom. But for those cases where the evidence is fairly contained and certain, the iPad app is a great option.

The TrialDirector app gives you two ways to get exhibits and other information onto your iPad: Dropbox or iTunes. If you have created a case file in the TrialDirector desktop application, you can export the data into either Dropbox or iTunes, and then move it onto the iPad from one of those locations. However, you are not limited to using the desktop version of TrialDirector; you can use the iPad app as a stand-alone tool, much like the other apps above. **Note:** You cannot create folders in the TrialDirector app, so if you plan to organize your exhibits into folders, you will need to do that before you import them into the app.

Like other evidence presentation apps, TrialDirector gives you a decent set of annotation tools (see Figure 6.3). You can highlight or draw on exhibits; create circles, lines, or rectangles; redact portions of an exhibit; zoom and callout on documents or images; and review exhibits side by side. The app will display video, including depositions with synchronized transcripts, as well as just about any type of image. You can bookmark important exhibits, much like you designate Key Docs in TrialPad, so you can refer to them during closing or other critical moments of the trial. TrialDirector provides no way to export anything from the app. You can save an exhibit with its annotations, but that's about it. As of now, there's no way save your TrialDirector file back to Dropbox or iTunes once the trial is over.

Figure 6.3 TrialDirector for iPad

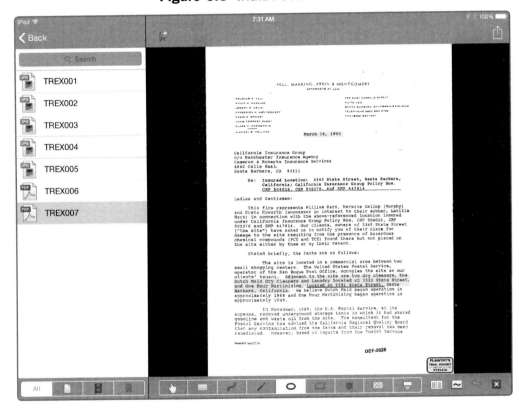

As a stand-alone trial presentation app, TrialDirector for iPad is decent. What makes it powerful is its connection to TrialDirector. On the other hand, it's free, and even an average app is okay if it's free. My recommendation, however, is to stick with TrialPad, unless (1) you have the desktop version of TrialDirector or (2) you like the idea of a free app.

Standard Presentation Apps

I have always been a firm believer that presentation tools like Power-Point and Keynote should only be used during the opening and closing phases of trial; those are the times you can prepare for in advance, without worrying that something will change while you are making your presentation. In contrast, using one of these tools while you are examining a witness can be fraught with peril, in the event that your witness does not answer as expected, or the judge suddenly rules inadmissible a portion of your line of questioning. That's why using an evidence presentation app like those mentioned above makes the most sense during the evidence portion of your trial. It allows you the flexibility to react on the fly to a witness's or judge's quirks, which almost always come up when you are presenting evidence.

However, I am all for using a traditional presentation app in opening and closing, because they offer certainty during a time when you need to focus more on the words coming out of your mouth than on what's happening with your technology. For those of you who live in the Microsoft Office universe, **PowerPoint for iPad** (http://bit.ly/1jApmPu) is a must-have app for giving a PowerPoint presentation. As I mentioned in Lesson 1, you must have a Microsoft Office 365 in order to use it, but I think that's an investment well worth making.

PowerPoint for iPad offers most of the tools in the desktop version, although as of this writing you cannot add or edit animations. But the app is great for giving presentations, with a Presenter View that allows you to annotate slides as you discuss them, as well as view any notes that you may have added to your slide deck (see Figure 6.4).

If you don't want to purchase an Office 365 subscription, your best option is one that most iPad users prefer, and that's **Keynote** (http://bit.ly/1tpbpI2). You can create presentations directly from your tablet, although you have access to only a limited number of templates (called Themes).

Figure 6.4 PowerPoint for iPad Presenter View

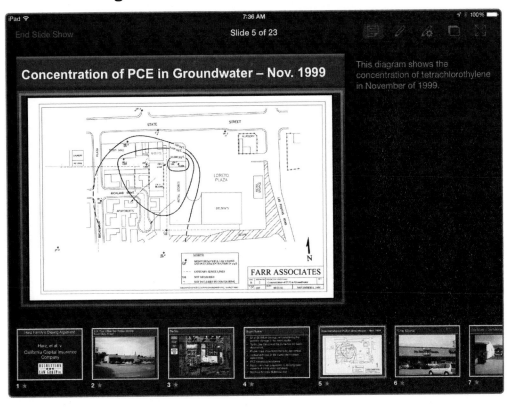

You can add slides in several different layouts, depending on the content you want to display. Adding bulleted text and applying basic formatting to your slides is simple, as is inserting photos, videos, tables, charts, or shapes (see Figure 6.5). The animations are fun and easy to build. Although the options in the iPad version of Keynote are not as robust as you might have on the Mac version, or even on the PC version of PowerPoint, you certainly have enough to put together a basic, professional-looking presentation. **Note:** If you use PowerPoint on the desktop, you can still use Keynote with your PowerPoint files—but it might not look exactly the same when you open it on your iPad. Keynote needs to convert the PowerPoint file to its own format, which may result in fonts being replaced or charts and tables altered. It can sometimes take a while to fix your presentation to get it back to its original condition. That's why I prefer to use PowerPoint on the iPad with my PowerPoint files.

Figure 6.5 Creating a Presentation in Keynote

Taking Notes at Trial

If you aren't questioning a witness or arguing the law to the judge at trial, then you're likely in your seat taking notes. The apps you used to take notes during the client intake phase of the case will work equally well at trial; again, it depends on your preferred method of note-taking. No matter whether you prefer to write by hand, type with a keyboard, or record the testimony as it occurs, there's an app for you. Check out Lesson 1 for my recommended note-taking apps.

The final app all lawyers should have in the courtroom is **BT Chat HD** (http://bit.ly/10at8bI), a free app that allows you to keep in touch with your trial team without saying a word. Once the app is installed on your iPad or iPhone, you can connect to the devices of others on your team by Bluetooth and chat in a private, secure chat room. The app is better to use than text messages, because having a text message appear across your screen when you are presenting evidence can be embarrassing. It's also better than an instant messaging app like Skype, because you never know when your Internet connection is going to fail. The app may also spell the end of sticky notes in trial. Now you no longer need to pass notes across the table to communicate with others on your team.

In this lesson, we have spent most of our time on the "what" of litigating *Davis v. ACME Industries* on the iPad—the apps you need to become an effective presenter of evidence in trial or at a hearing. We'll cover the "how" of presenting in court in the next lesson, where you will hear from experts who will give their best advice on using a tablet in court without having the judge yell or a jury laugh at you.

Tips from the Trenches:
Using the iPad in Court

For a trial technologist in the courtroom, the number one rule has to be "Don't embarrass the lawyers in front of the judge or jury." When technology goes wrong during trial, it is a distraction, and it can quickly become annoying to anyone who has to endure delays while the team works out the problems. That's why you must be fully prepared for any technology problems when you walk into the courtroom and ready to deal with a crisis if one arises.

It should be no different when you use an iPad. If you plan to use a tablet in presenting a case to the jury, you must be prepared. And *preparation* can mean a lot of different things. Over the past few years, lawyers in growing numbers have started using the iPad in court for trials and hearings. I wanted the final lesson in this book to come, in part, from them. After all, they are living proof that using an iPad in court is possible, with the right preparation.

Many of the tips in this lesson come from the following iPad experts:

- **Jamie Moncus**, a trial lawyer with Hare, Wynn, Newell & Newton in Birmingham, Alabama.
- **Spencer Farris**, a trial lawyer with the S.E. Farris Law Firm in St. Louis, Missouri.

- **Frank King**, an Assistant Attorney General with the Texas Office of the Attorney General.
- **Drew Harris**, an Assistant Attorney General with the Texas Office of the Attorney General.
- **Ann Jacobs**, a trial lawyer with Jacobs Injury Law in Milwaukee, Wisconsin.
- **Kenneth Laska**, a trial lawyer with Segal & Laska in Plainville, Connecticut.

Courtroom Setup and Equipment

Our trial lawyers all had good advice on choosing the right equipment and setting it up in the courtroom.

Wi-Fi. All the experts advised against reliance on courtroom Wi-Fi throughout the duration of a trial. The connection might be weak to begin with, but even with a strong signal, you never know when someone in the courtroom might decide to download a video or otherwise compromise the signal. If you need Internet access, make sure you have your own hotspot available, and if you are using Apple TV or AirServer, pack a router so you don't have to worry about an Internet connection at all. I currently use the **MiFi Jetpack** (available from Verizon, AT&T, and other carriers) for a portable Internet connection and have been very satisfied with its coverage and signal strength. You can also use your cell phone as a hotspot if your wireless plan supports it.

Cables. If you plan to use your iPad with a VGA adapter, keep a long (10- to 15-foot) VGA cable available for use with a projector. In many courtrooms, the VGA connection to the projector is short, or taped down, and as a result you may find yourself tethered to the projector throughout the trial. With an extension VGA cord, you give yourself greater freedom to work at the witness stand, podium, or counsel table, or move around the courtroom in general. The military slogan "two is one; one is none" resonates with our experts, who prefer to have several cables available in court in case of emergency.

One other tip if you still happen to be using an older model iPad, with the 30-pin VGA dongle: don't move around too much. The VGA dongle itself is a good argument for why you should purchase the latest iPad and use the Lightning VGA adapter. The 30-pin dongle is too short, and it tends to disconnect very easily from the iPad. When it does, the projector loses the signal, and you'll probably find yourself waiting a few seconds for the projector to find it again. With some projectors, this can take an uncomfortably long time. If moving around is unavoidable, make sure you carry a supply of professional gaffer tape in your equipment bag, and use a strip of tape to anchor the VGA adapter to your iPad.

Charging your iPad. An iPad has a relatively long battery life, often lasting ten hours on one charge. But if you are using the iPad through-out the day, you may drain the battery faster than you might expect. Further, if you're using the VGA adapter to present, you won't be able to charge your iPad at all during that time. Make sure you start out the day with a full charge, and connect the iPad to your charger whenever you aren't using it. For those courtrooms where a power outlet is not readily available, consider bringing a portable charger to use during the day. Spencer Farris swears by the **ZaggSparq** (http://bit.ly/1tVmUbN); I like just about any charger made by Anker, including the **Astro3** (http://bit.ly/1uoAO8p), which features outlets to charge your iPad as well as your phone or other devices.

Even if you don't bring a dedicated charger for your iPad, bring a power strip with multiple outlets so you have a place to plug in your regular iPad charging cord. Older courthouses are notorious for either having too few outlets or unreliable ones, so find one outlet that works and plug all of your devices into a power strip that contains a surge protector.

Stylus. More than one of our experts reported losing a stylus while in trial. If you are the type to lose pens, you may also find yourself scrambling to find your stylus when you need to jot down important witness testimony. Head over to Amazon and buy some really cheap styli; you can buy a pack of ten for less than five dollars. They may not work as well as the higher-priced models, but they will do in a pinch.

Other equipment. When it comes to your own evidence, your goal is to have everything you need loaded on your iPad, with all of your other case files in electronic format in Dropbox or some other location. But what if opposing counsel hands you a paper exhibit that you'd like to present yourself? The easiest solution is to use a scanning app like **Scanner Pro** or **Genius Scan** (http://bit.ly/1GilFsu) to scan the document directly into your iPad. If you have a lot of documents to scan, it might make sense to have a portable scanner on hand to scan those exhibits to a Dropbox account. If you're interested in a light, inexpensive portable scanner, try one of the fantastic Fujitsu ScanSnap models; both the iX100 (http://bit.ly/10gCBye) and the S1100 (http://bit.ly/PM7G7h) models are good current portable choices.

Be prepared. Finally, the experts could not stress enough the importance of testing your equipment before the trial starts. Ideally, you'll have time to visit the courtroom at least a day before you're scheduled to start. By testing your equipment ahead of time, you give yourself the opportunity to fix any problems that arise or buy any additional equipment you may need.

Being prepared also means getting into the courtroom well in advance of trial so you can get set up. It's a good idea to make sure the judge and opposing counsel are aware of your intention to use technology in the courtroom so there are no surprises. And there's nothing worse than making a judge or jury wait while you set up your equipment. Make sure it's ready to go by the time the judge sits down at the bench.

Apps and iPad Use in General

When dealing with the iPad and its various apps, our experts gave these recommendations.

Stick with one app. Avoid using more than one app at a time. In other words, don't use TrialPad, and then switch out to PDF Expert to show a PDF file or a video app to show a video. Although the newer iPads are pretty fast, switching between apps can be distracting for a jury. Sticking with one app is especially important for opening and closing argument; I think it is a mistake to use both TrialPad or some other evidence presentation app (for showing specific exhibits) *and* Keynote or PowerPoint for a more structured presentation. Use one or the other.

Use an evidence presentation app if your presentation will be heavy on showing exhibits, and Keynote/PowerPoint if you will be giving more of a persuasive presentation. If you need to show exhibits, you can always insert digital images of the documents into your Keynote or Power-Point presentation.

Update at the right time. A corollary to the "Be Prepared" rule above involves the apps themselves: *Never update an app right before you go into court.* It's always nice to see an update to an app arrive on your iPad, and I know I am always looking forward to trying out new features that might be included. But until you can test out the update, you cannot be sure whether the new features will affect the way you currently use the app, or even if features you rely on in your presentation have been removed from or altered in the new version. If you see that an update is available the night before trial begins, resist the urge to update until after trial is over.

Turn off notifications. One of the great features of the iPad is its Notifications Center. You can use it to configure each app to notify you when something happens—when an email or text message arrives, when your friends update their Facebook pages, or even when your favorite sports team scores. Needless to say, having any of these notifications pop up on screen when presenting to a jury is distracting at best and unprofessional at worst. Before going to trial, visit **Settings > Notifications** and make sure they are all set to **OFF**. Unfortunately, there's not a global OFF button, so you'll need to go into each app that's listed in the **Notifications** Center and turn **Allow Notifications OFF**.

A related problem comes when your battery gets low. When the iPad battery drains to 20 percent, a message will appear on your screen, and then again when there is 10 percent battery life remaining. There's nothing you can do to turn this notification off, and it's not really the best message you want to send to a jury, so try to avoid draining your battery to the 20 percent level during a given day (see Charging Your iPad, above).

Organize files and documents. Give some thought ahead of time to the naming conventions for your files and folders, and set up your filing structure before starting to load exhibits. If you throw all of your documents into an evidence presentation app without a thoughtful plan, you will spend a lot of extra time getting organized within the app.

Even better, organize your Dropbox folders the same way, so you can easily find the documents you need, whether they are on your iPad or in Dropbox. You might consider naming folders after the phases of trial. Creating folders for Voir Dire, Opening, Closing, and individual witnesses will help you to be more organized during the trial.

Plan for *all* the evidence you might present, not just the exhibits you plan to introduce during your case in chief. If you know a witness is going to respond a certain way, plan to have your impeachment deposition excerpts or other piece of evidence ready for cross-examination.

Before you get to court, convert all of your case files to electronic format so you don't have to keep switching between paper and electronic. If you received paper discovery from opposing counsel or other parties, scan everything well in advance of trial and organize it along with all of your other electronic files. If you have odd-sized photos or documents, take care to scan them so that you don't cut off part of the image, or have to otherwise manipulate the image to make it presentable to a jury. That said, be prepared to do just that, in the event you have digital images that would be difficult for a jury to read or understand. For easy photo editing, I like **Adobe Photoshop Express** (http://bit.ly/1p2EgO7). The editing tools are easy to use, and the app is free.

Some of our experts also recommended going through your exhibits and individually testing them to make sure there are no surprises when you present them to a jury. With some apps, larger files can cause "redraw" problems when you show them on the iPad (this means that the iPad screen will take some time to properly display the exhibit). Identify any problem files, and either fix them or have a plan for bringing them up on your iPad without the jury's notice.

When presenting evidence from an iPad, take a moment when you are highlighting or "pulling out" from an onscreen exhibit; give the jury time to soak up the evidence you are presenting. Opposing counsel may even ask you to leave an exhibit up on your iPad so they can use it during their examination.

Have a backup. The experts all agreed on the importance of having a backup plan. But backup can mean different things. Having a duplicate copy of all your exhibits is important; some recommend having a separate iPad loaded with the same apps and documents in the event your primary iPad should fail. As a last resort, be prepared with paper copies of your exhibits in case all of your technology goes bad. Hope for the best, but prepare for the worst.

Practice, practice, practice. Although the iPad is not a difficult device to learn, you *must* understand how the apps you're going to use work before you walk through the courtroom door. Set up your iPad with a projector and screen and learn to present evidence with TrialPad, or practice giving your opening statement using Keynote or PowerPoint. The best trial lawyers are successful because they prepare, and that includes the technology they use as well.

Finally, don't try to use more technology than makes you comfortable. Trying a case is hard enough; if you're having trouble understanding how the technology works, don't kill yourself trying to make it happen. Find someone—an assistant, paralegal, associate, or hired technologist—who can handle the technology for you.

State Rules/Statutes Available as of Publication

Note: Some of the apps below have not been updated in several years. Before using an app, confirm that it has the most recent statutory/rule updates for that particular jurisdiction.

Alabama

- Alabama Code (2012 edition) aka AL12 (http://bit.ly/1ua8a8W)
- Alabama Rules of Civil Procedure 2011 (http://bit.ly/1owpJ2u)
- The Code of Alabama (http://bit.ly/1qw1EEy)

Alaska

- Alaska Courts (http://bit.ly/1tN0A2M)
- Alaska Statutes (2012 edition) aka AK12 (http://bit.ly/1wF5fpP)

Arizona

- Arizona Revised Statutes (http://bit.ly/1zapDyv)
- Arizona Statutes (2012 edition) aka ARS12 (http://bit.ly/1qw2uRM)
- LawBox (http://bit.ly/1zCU6YV)

Arkansas

- Arkansas Code of 1987 ARCode09 (http://bit.ly/1uNBT9O)

California

- CA Law (All 29 California State Codes/Statutes) (http://bit.ly/1pBHPkt)
- CA Law–2014 (All 29 Codes of California Laws) (http://bit.ly/1EeNJZK)
- CA Laws (All 29 Codes and Rules) (http://bit.ly/1zaqgbi)
- California Appellate Rules (http://bit.ly/1xop6cM)
- CA Business & Professions Code 2014 (http://bit.ly/1EsNsnX)
- CA Civil Code 2014 (http://bit.ly/118ewea)
- CA Civil Rules (CA Labor Code 2014 (http://bit.ly/1GC8jaH)
- CA Code of Civil Procedure 2014 (http://bit.ly/1zEpBSm)
- CA Evidence Code (http://bit.ly/1zCVSJI)
- CA Evidence Code 2014 (http://bit.ly/1tUJZf1)
- CA Fish & Game Code 2014 (http://bit.ly/1oyOn2t)
- CA Labor Code 2014 (http://bit.ly/1GC8jaH)
- California Family & Juvenile Rules (http://bit.ly/1EeQGcP)
- CA Family Code (http://bit.ly/1tN4sAP)
- CA Family Code 2014 (http://bit.ly/1owu5Xd)
- CA Harbors & Navigation Code 2012 (http://bit.ly/1zEpK8A)
- CA Health and Safety Code (http://bit.ly/1qw4No2)
- CA Health & Safety Code 2014 (http://bit.ly/1ttXkWo)
- California Courts (http://bit.ly/1xgtPwb)
- California Criminal Rules (http://bit.ly/140geiW)

- California Probate Rules (http://bit.ly/1uRxHpy)
- California Rules of Court (Titles 1–10) (http://bit.ly/1uNIrFC)
- CA Penal Code (http://bit.ly/1qw32XL)
- CA Penal Code 2014 (http://bit.ly/1zCV8nL)
- CA Probate Code 2014 (http://bit.ly/1xaVjWC)
- CA Trial Court Rules (http://bit.ly/1ttS9Wy)
- CA Vehicle Code (http://bit.ly/10JlK7O)
- CA Vehicle Code 2014 (http://bit.ly/10DYl7i)
- CA Welfare & Institutions Code 2014 (http://bit.ly/1uceDQS)
- LawBox (http://bit.ly/1zCU6YV)
- LawStack (http://bit.ly/1uIEHmy)
- Rulebook (http://bit.ly/1tgxNXf)

Colorado
- Colorado Rules of Civil Procedure 2011 (http://bit.ly/1zcv7IT)
- Rulebook (http://bit.ly/1tgxNXf)

Connecticut
- Conn Courts (http://bit.ly/1xxZc4x)
- Connecticut General Statutes aka CT11 (http://bit.ly/1uchJnU)

Delaware
- Delaware Code (http://bit.ly/1xxZI2u)
- Delaware Code (http://bit.ly/1zErGOd)
- Delaware Courts (http://bit.ly/1xbTKHX)
- eDelaware (http://bit.ly/1ymmJFF)

- Morris Nichols' Delaware Bankruptcy Companion (http://bit.ly/1ymmOco)
- Morris Nichols' Delaware Trust Law Companion (http://bit.ly/1zcw83S)
- Rulebook (http://bit.ly/1tgxNXf)

Florida

- FL Law (http://bit.ly/1ucnWAh)
- FL Criminal Code 2014 (http://bit.ly/1AN1Vgf)
- Florida Criminal Code (http://bit.ly/1xj7kH6)
- Florida Criminal Procedure and Corrections Code (http://bit.ly/1xoz9P1)
- Florida Evidence Code (http://bit.ly/1oz0mx4)
- Florida Family Law Rules of Procedure (http://bit.ly/1xoyH3h)
- FL Motor Vehicles Code 2014 (http://bit.ly/118nXdH)
- Florida Motor Vehicles Code (http://bit.ly/118mZ1b)
- Florida Rules (http://bit.ly/1qxXVX7)
- Florida Rules of Civil Procedure (http://bit.ly/1uRMbWt)
- Florida Statutes (http://bit.ly/1tQbFjD)
- Florida Statutes (http://bit.ly/1zEv5g7)
- LawBox (http://bit.ly/1zCU6YV)
- Rulebook (http://bit.ly/1tgxNXf)

Georgia

- Georgia Courts (http://bit.ly/1ucoXbB)
- Rulebook (http://bit.ly/1tgxNXf)

Hawaii

- (No iPad apps as of this writing)

Idaho

- Idaho Code aka ID12 (http://bit.ly/1OHmKsA)

Illinois

- ICS Law (Illinois Compiled Statutes) (http://bit.ly/1xjDjqr)
- IL Courts (http://bit.ly/1EteFab)
- IL Law (http://bit.ly/1zd3W0D)
- Illinois Criminal Law (http://bit.ly/1zd41RT)
- Illinois Transportation Law (http://bit.ly/1zd3W0D)
- LawBox (http://bit.ly/1zCU6YV)
- Rulebook (http://bit.ly/1tgxNXf)

Indiana

- Rulebook (http://bit.ly/1tgxNXf)

Iowa

- Iowa Code 2012 aka IA12 (http://bit.ly/1ozCqcI)
- Iowa Code (http://bit.ly/1GFdre1)

Kansas

- Kansas Statutes (http://bit.ly/1w66DOh)

Kentucky

- (No iPad apps as of this writing)

Louisiana

- LA Law (http://bit.ly/1stHbAW)
- LA Civil Code (http://bit.ly/1stHbAW)

- LA Code of Civil Procedure (http://bit.ly/1xyYt2Y)
- LA Code of Criminal Procedure (http://bit.ly/1uPhAbG)
- LA Code of Evidence (http://bit.ly/1ozE2Di)
- LA Courts (http://bit.ly/1ucWUZC)
- LA Criminal Code 2014 (http://bit.ly/1uPie97)
- LA Children's Code (http://bit.ly/1zd65cC)
- LA Children's Code 2011 (http://bit.ly/1tYnIgi)
- LA Motor Vehicles & Traffic Regulation 2014 (http://bit.ly/1w69kPK)
- LA Public Health & Safety 2011 (http://bit.ly/1w69kPK)
- Louisiana Civil Code (http://bit.ly/1FQgJNE)
- Louisiana Code of Civil Procedure (http://bit.ly/1xyYt2Y)
- Louisiana Supreme Court Rules (http://bit.ly/1sonEB1)

Maine

- (No iPad apps as of this writing)

Maryland

- Rulebook (http://bit.ly/1tgxNXf)

Massachusetts

- MA Law (http://bit.ly/1AQsph1)
- General Laws of Massachusetts (http://bit.ly/1tS5kEn)
- MA Penal Code (http://bit.ly/1uUaIdN)
- MA Vehicle Code (http://bit.ly/1uUazXN)
- Mass Courts (http://bit.ly/1GGg9Qy)
- Rulebook (http://bit.ly/1tgxNXf)

Michigan
- Mich Courts (http://bit.ly/1w7Mhny)
- Michigan Laws (http://bit.ly/1tS5Zpi)
- MI Law (http://bit.ly/1sutm5t)
- Rulebook (http://bit.ly/1tgxNXf)

Minnesota
- MN Law—Animal Cruelty (http://bit.ly/1uUcgV8)
- MN Law—Criminal Law (http://bit.ly/1zdWQsI)
- MN Law—Juvenile Law (http://bit.ly/1AQvflW)
- MN Law—Motor Vehicle Law (http://bit.ly/1spI0tD)

Mississippi
- (No iPad apps as of this writing)

Missouri
- Missouri Revised Statutes (http://bit.ly/1yolvKe)
- MO Law (http://bit.ly/1EtT55t)
- Rulebook (http://bit.ly/1tgxNXf)

Montana
- (No iPad apps as of this writing)

Nebraska
- Nebraska Revised Statutes (http://bit.ly/1Ej5FCw)
- NEStatutes09 (http://bit.ly/1zdXere)

Nevada

- Nevada Revised Statutes aka NRS10 (http://bit.ly/1uUsxsg)

New Hampshire

- New Hampshire Statutes (http://bit.ly/1uXjnfm)

New Jersey

- New Jersey Permanent Statutes (NJ12) (http://bit.ly/1uXjnfm)
- New Jersey Statutes and Codes (http://bit.ly/1pJFPqo)
- NJ Law (http://bit.ly/1zHw4fx)
- NJ Law–Title 2C–Criminal Law (http://bit.ly/1xdKgfb)
- NJ Law–Title 10–Civil Rights (http://bit.ly/1swGh6T)
- NJ Law–Title 39–Motor Vehicle (http://bit.ly/1xsihHi)
- Rulebook (http://bit.ly/1tgxNXf)

New Mexico

- (No iPad apps as of this writing)

New York

- LawBox (http://bit.ly/1zCU6YV)
- LawStack (http://bit.ly/1uIEHmy)
- New York Laws (http://bit.ly/1wbLan3)
- New York Statutes (http://bit.ly/11c7EfS)
- NY Alcoholic Beverage Control Law 2014 (http://bit.ly/1oDtAKZ)
- NY Civil Practice Law and Rules (http://bit.ly/1u2BRJo)
- NY Civil Practice Law and Rules 2014 (http://bit.ly/1xdL3wC)
- NY Civil Service Law 2013 (http://bit.ly/145xgw8)

- NY Code of Criminal Procedure (http://bit.ly/1EvrKQm)
- NY Criminal Procedure Law 2014 (http://bit.ly/1xsjxKx)
- NY Domestic Relations Law 2014 (http://bit.ly/1zHycUv)
- NY Estates, Powers and Trusts Law 2014 (http://bit.ly/1qAVN0T)
- NY Family Court Act 2014 (http://bit.ly/1xE6fsv)
- NY Judiciary Law 2014 (http://bit.ly/1wbO0sb)
- NY Law (http://bit.ly/1uXl78q)
- NY Penal Code (http://bit.ly/1xE3ZBw)
- NY Penal Law 2014 (http://bit.ly/1u2APx7)
- NY SCPA 2014 (http://bit.ly/1ssYlxF)
- NY Vehicle and Traffic Code (http://bit.ly/1GJ5hkS)
- NY Vehicle and Traffic Law 2014 (http://bit.ly/1xsjq1r)
- NY Vehicle and Traffic Law (http://bit.ly/1ug9uqX)
- Rulebook (http://bit.ly/1tgxNXf)

North Carolina
- LawStack (http://bit.ly/1uIEHmy)
- NC12 North Carolina General Statutes (http://bit.ly/1qAWqaG)
- NCLaw—Animal Cruelty (http://bit.ly/1wbPy5n)
- NCLaw—Criminal Law (http://bit.ly/1qAWrLI)
- NCLaw—Motor Vehicle (http://bit.ly/1uXoOuL)
- North Carolina General Statutes (http://bit.ly/1tVh7Sk)
- North Carolina General Statutes (http://bit.ly/1zHz8bm)

North Dakota
- North Dakota Century Code (2009 Edition) (http://bit.ly/1uXp7pu)

Ohio

- Ohio Revised Code (http://bit.ly/1st1qxF)
- Ohio Revised Code (http://bit.ly/1ugccN3)
- Ohio Revised Code aka OH11 (http://bit.ly/1uXprEK)
- Rulebook (http://bit.ly/1tgxNXf)

Oklahoma

- Oklahoma Courts (http://bit.ly/1GJ8CQS)
- OK12 Oklahoma Statutes (http://bit.ly/1xmZVGF)
- Oklahoma Statutes (http://bit.ly/11cbAgQ)

Oregon

- LawStack (http://bit.ly/1uIEHmy)
- Oregon Courts (http://bit.ly/1u2GlzR)
- Oregon Law (http://bit.ly/1EmedZw)
- ORS12 State of Oregon Revised Statutes (http://bit.ly/1swKMyf)
- Oregon Revised Statutes (http://bit.ly/1swKIi7)
- Rulebook (http://bit.ly/1tgxNXf)

Pennsylvania

- PALaw Title 18—Criminal Law (http://bit.ly/1wc1Drf)
- PALaw Title 75—Vehicle Code (http://bit.ly/1qB1kV6)
- PA Rules of Appellate Procedure (http://bit.ly/1zfETdq)
- PA Rules—Juvenile Court Procedure (http://bit.ly/1ugkmoM)

Rhode Island

- (No iPad apps as of this writing)

South Carolina

- South Carolina Code of Laws aka SC10 (http://bit.ly/10SeIgR)

South Dakota

- South Dakota Codified Laws aka SD09 (http://bit.ly/1stfLKK)

Tennessee

- Tennessee Laws (http://bit.ly/1xstuaJ)
- TN12 Tennessee Code (http://bit.ly/1tzMcHr)

Texas

- LawBox (http://bit.ly/1zCU6YV)
- LawStack (http://bit.ly/1uIEHmy)
- Rulebook (http://bit.ly/1tgxNXf)
- Texas 2012 Code aka TX12 (http://bit.ly/1pJZaYB)
- Texas Bar Legal (http://bit.ly/1GJrsHD)
- Texas Courts (http://bit.ly/1swRBjr)
- Texas Rules of Appellate Procedure (http://bit.ly/1qB340t)
- Texas Rules of Civil Procedure (http://bit.ly/1AWyad4)
- Texas Rules of Evidence (http://bit.ly/1oDHixy)
- Texas Statutes (http://bit.ly/1uUPCLq)
- TX Code of Criminal Procedure (http://bit.ly/1swRVyv)
- TX Code of Criminal Procedure 2014 (http://bit.ly/1tzNUsl)
- TX Family Code (http://bit.ly/1oDHkWm)
- TX Family Code 2014 (http://bit.ly/1xn9DZE)
- TX Health and Safety Code (http://bit.ly/1wMhPDE)
- TX Health & Safety Code 2014 (http://bit.ly/1qB2WOz)

- TX Laws (http://bit.ly/1uUPCLq)
- TX Penal Code (http://bit.ly/1GJhGW0)
- TX Penal Code 2014 (http://bit.ly/1uUQBLF)
- TX Probate Code (http://bit.ly/1wc5RiI)
- TX Rules of Civil Procedure (http://bit.ly/1AWyad4)
- TX Transportation Code (http://bit.ly/1pJXLkD)
- TX Transportation Code 2014 (http://bit.ly/1tVurpD)

Utah

- Rulebook (http://bit.ly/1tgxNXf)
- Utah Code (http://bit.ly/1yryJpx)
- Utah Code (http://bit.ly/1u2S0hY)
- Utah Code/Statutes aka UT11 (http://bit.ly/1xdRYpR)

Vermont

- VT12 Vermont Statutes (http://bit.ly/1wc7A7G)

Virginia

- Code of Virginia (http://bit.ly/1stkj3M)
- Code of Virginia (http://bit.ly/1EvDUZD)
- Rulebook (http://bit.ly/1tgxNXf)

Washington

- LawStack (http://bit.ly/1uIEHmy)
- RCW2012 Revised Code of Washington (http://bit.ly/11cnjf6)
- Revised Code of Washington (http://bit.ly/1qB444O)

- Rulebook (http://bit.ly/1tgxNXf)
- WA Law (http://bit.ly/1xdSPGN)
- Washington Courts (http://bit.ly/1wMjOb1)

West Virginia
- (No iPad apps as of this writing)

Wisconsin
- (No iPad apps as of this writing)

Wyoming
- WY09 Wyoming Statutes 2009 (http://bit.ly/1oDKTeU)

Setting Up a Dropbox Account

It's easy to set up a cloud storage account like Dropbox, Box or OneDrive. Here are the basic steps to get started, using Dropbox as an example:

- Visit www.dropbox.com and click ***Create an Account***.

- Once you register, you'll be prompted to download the Dropbox software.

- When the installation is complete, you'll see a new folder called **Dropbox**. Add a file or folder to the Dropbox folder, and it will be automatically synced to Dropbox's servers.

- If you want to access your synchronized files on another computer, repeat the second step, above. Instead of registering, you'll be asked to sign in with your email and password. Once you log in, this computer is now connected to your Dropbox account (**Note:** While you're registering, it's a great idea to enable **Two-Factor Authentication** for added security.)

- You'll see a similar folder called Dropbox on your computer. Open it and you'll see the files you added to your other computer back in the third step, above. That's how Dropbox works—by making sure you have an up-to-date copy of all your files on every computer you use.

- Now add any files you want to synchronize with other computers, and you will be able to access them anywhere, including your iPad.

- You can access your Dropbox folders on your iPad in two ways. First, download the Dropbox app (http://bit.ly/10Snpbf). Once you log in, you'll see all the files you loaded into your Dropbox folder on your other computers. I don't use the Dropbox app all the time, though, because most of the apps I use automatically connect to Dropbox. Just go to the ***Settings*** menu in any app you want to connect, and if a Dropbox connection is available, you'll be able to enter your login credentials there and get connected.

- You can securely share any of your Dropbox files with others, or even an entire folder (see Figure A.1). On your computer, right-click the file or Dropbox folder you want to share; if you're sharing a file, select ***Share Dropbox Link***. You'll get a link to the file that you can paste into an email, text, or other location. To share a folder, select ***Share This Folder***. You'll be taken to the Dropbox website, where you can enter the email addresses of those with whom you are sharing the folder. Your recipients will all get links to the folder, and soon they can access it on their own.

Figure A.1 Sharing Files in Dropbox

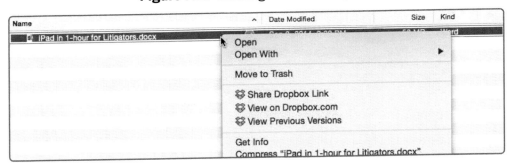

Index

SELECTED BOOKS FROM THE LAW PRACTICE DIVISION

LinkedIn in One Hour for Lawyers, Second Edition
By Dennis Kennedy and Allison C. Shields

Product Code: 5110773 • **LPM Price:** $39.95 • **Regular Price:** $49.95

Since the first edition of LinkedIn in One Hour for Lawyers was published, LinkedIn has added almost 100 million users, and more and more lawyers are using the platform on a regular basis. Now, this bestselling ABA book has been fully revised and updated to reflect significant changes to LinkedIn's layout and functionality made through 2013. LinkedIn in One Hour for Lawyers, Second Edition, will help lawyers make the most of their online professional networking. In just one hour, you will learn to:

- Set up a LinkedIn® account
- Create a robust, dynamic profile--and take advantage of new multimedia options
- Build your connections
- Get up to speed on new features such as Endorsements, Influencers, Contacts, and Channels
- Enhance your Company Page with new functionality
- Use search tools to enhance your network
- Monitor your network with ease
- Optimize your settings for privacy concerns
- Use LinkedIn® effectively in the hiring process
- Develop a LinkedIn strategy to grow your legal network

Blogging in One Hour for Lawyers
By Ernie Svenson

Product Code: 5110744 • **LPM Price:** $24.95 • **Regular Price:** $39.95

Until a few years ago, only the largest firms could afford to engage an audience of millions. Now, lawyers in any size firm can reach a global audience at little to no cost—all because of blogs. An effective blog can help you promote your practice, become more "findable" online, and take charge of how you are perceived by clients, journalists and anyone who uses the Internet. Blogging in One Hour for Lawyers will show you how to create, maintain, and improve a legal blog—and gain new business opportunities along the way. In just one hour, you will learn to:

- Set up a blog quickly and easily
- Write blog posts that will attract clients
- Choose from various hosting options like Blogger, TypePad, and WordPress
- Make your blog friendly to search engines, increasing your ranking
- Tweak the design of your blog by adding customized banners and colors
- Easily send notice of your blog posts to Facebook and Twitter
- Monitor your blog's traffic with Google Analytics and other tools
- Avoid ethics problems that may result from having a legal blog

The Electronic Evidence and Discovery Handbook: Forms, Checklists, and Guidelines
By Sharon D. Nelson, Bruce A. Olson, and John W. Simek

Product Code: 5110569 • **LPM Price:** $99.95 • **Regular Price:** $129.95

The use of electronic evidence has increased dramatically over the past few years, but many lawyers still struggle with the complexities of electronic discovery. This substantial book provides lawyers with the templates they need to frame their discovery requests and provides helpful advice on what they can subpoena. In addition to the ready-made forms, the authors also supply explanations to bring you up to speed on the electronic discovery field. The accompanying CD-ROM features over 70 forms, including, Motions for Protective Orders, Preservation and Spoliation Documents, Motions to Compel, Electronic Evidence Protocol Agreements, Requests for Production, Internet Services Agreements, and more. Also included is a full electronic evidence case digest with over 300 cases detailed!

Facebook® in One Hour for Lawyers
By Dennis Kennedy and Allison C. Shields

Product Code: 5110745 • **LPM Price:** $24.95 • **Regular Price:** $39.95

With a few simple steps, lawyers can use Facebook® to market their services, grow their practices, and expand their legal network—all by using the same methods they already use to communicate with friends and family. *Facebook® in One Hour for Lawyers* will show any attorney—from Facebook® novices to advanced users—how to use this powerful tool for both professional and personal purposes.

Android Apps in One Hour for Lawyers
By Daniel J. Siegel

Product Code: 5110754 • **LPM Price:** $19.95 • **Regular Price:** $34.95

Lawyers are already using Android devices to make phone calls, check e-mail, and send text messages. After the addition of several key apps, Android smartphones or tablets can also help run a law practice. From the more than 800,000 apps currently available, Android Apps in One Hour for Lawyers highlights the "best of the best" apps that will allow you to practice law from your mobile device. In just one hour, this book will describe how to buy, install, and update Android apps, and help you:

- Store documents and files in the cloud
- Use security apps to safeguard client data on your phone
- Be organized and productive with apps for to-do lists, calendar, and contacts
- Communicate effectively with calling, text, and e-mail apps
- Create, edit, and organize your documents
- Learn on the go with news, reading, and reference apps
- Download utilities to keep your device running smoothly
- Hit the road with apps for travel
- Have fun with games and social media apps

TO ORDER VISIT **WWW.SHOPABA.ORG** OR CALL 1-800-285-2221

Virtual Law Practice: How to Deliver Legal Services Online
By Stephanie L. Kimbro

Product Code: 5110707 • **LPM Price:** $47.95 • **Regular Price:** $79.95

The legal market has recently experienced a dramatic shift as lawyers seek out alternative methods of practicing law and providing more affordable legal services. Virtual law practice is revolutionizing the way the public receives legal services and how legal professionals work with clients. If you are interested in this form of practicing law, *Virtual Law Practice* will help you:

- Responsibly deliver legal services online to your clients
- Successfully set up and operate a virtual law office
- Establish a virtual law practice online through a secure, client-specific portal
- Manage and market your virtual law practice
- Understand state ethics and advisory opinions
- Find more flexibility and work/life balance in the legal profession

Social Media for Lawyers: The Next Frontier
By Carolyn Elefant and Nicole Black

Product Code: 5110710 • **LPM Price:** $47.95 • **Regular Price:** $79.95

The world of legal marketing has changed with the rise of social media sites such as Linkedin, Twitter, and Facebook. Law firms are seeking their companies attention with tweets, videos, blog posts, pictures, and online content. Social media is fast and delivers news at record pace. This book provides you with a practical, goal-centric approach to using social media in your law practice that will enable you to identify social media platforms and tools that fit your practice and implement them easily, efficiently, and ethically.

iPad Apps in One Hour for Lawyers
By Tom Mighell

Product Code: 5110739 • **LPM Price:** $19.95 • **Regular Price:** $34.95

At last count, there were more than 80,000 apps available for the iPad. Finding the best apps often can be an overwhelming, confusing, and frustrating process. iPad Apps in One Hour for Lawyers provides the "best of the best" apps that are essential for any law practice. In just one hour, you will learn about the apps most worthy of your time and attention. This book will describe how to buy, install, and update iPad apps, and help you:

- Find apps to get organized and improve your productivity
- Create, manage, and store documents on your iPad
- Choose the best apps for your law office, including litigation and billing apps
- Find the best news, reading, and reference apps
- Take your iPad on the road with apps for travelers
- Maximize your social networking power
- Have some fun with game and entertainment apps during your relaxation time

Twitter in One Hour for Lawyers
By Jared Correia

Product Code: 5110746 • **LPM Price:** $24.95 • **Regular Price:** $39.95

More lawyers than ever before are using Twitter to network with colleagues, attract clients, market their law firms, and even read the news. But to the uninitiated, Twitter's short messages, or tweets, can seem like they are written in a foreign language. Twitter in One Hour for Lawyers will demystify one of the most important social-media platforms of our time and teach you to tweet like an expert. In just one hour, you will learn to:

- Create a Twitter account and set up your profile
- Read tweets and understand Twitter jargon
- Write tweets—and send them at the appropriate time
- Gain an audience—follow and be followed
- Engage with other Twitters users
- Integrate Twitter into your firm's marketing plan
- Cross-post your tweets with other social media platforms like Facebook and LinkedIn
- Understand the relevant ethics, privacy, and security concerns
- Get the greatest possible return on your Twitter investment
- And much more!

The Lawyer's Essential Guide to Writing
By Marie Buckley

Product Code: 5110726 • **LPM Price:** $47.95 • **Regular Price:** $79.95

This is a readable, concrete guide to contemporary legal writing. Based on Marie Buckley's years of experience coaching lawyers, this book provides a systematic approach to all forms of written communication, from memoranda and briefs to e-mail and blogs. The book sets forth three principles for powerful writing and shows how to apply those principles to develop a clean and confident style.

iPad in One Hour for Lawyers, Third Edition
By Tom Mighell

Product Code: 5110779 • **LPM Price:** $39.95 • **Regular Price:** $49.95

Whether you are a new or a more advanced iPad user, *iPad in One Hour for Lawyers* takes a great deal of the mystery and confusion out of using your iPad. Ideal for lawyers who want to get up to speed swiftly, this book presents the essentials so you don't get bogged down in technical jargon and extraneous features and apps. In just six, short lessons, you'll learn how to:

- Quickly Navigate and Use the iPad User Interface
- Set Up Mail, Calendar, and Contacts
- Create and Use Folders to Multitask and Manage Apps
- Add Files to Your iPad, and Sync Them
- View and Manage Pleadings, Case Law, Contracts, and other Legal Documents
- Use Your iPad to Take Notes and Create Documents
- Use Legal-Specific Apps at Trial or in Doing Research

30-DAY RISK-FREE ORDER FORM

Please print or type. To ship UPS, we must have your street address.
If you list a P.O. Box, we will ship by U.S. Mail.

Name

Member ID

Firm/Organization

Street Address

City/State/Zip

Area Code/Phone (In case we have a question about your order)

E-mail

Method of Payment:
☐ Check enclosed, payable to American Bar Association
☐ MasterCard   ☐ Visa   ☐ American Express

Card Number   Expiration Date

Signature Required

MAIL THIS FORM TO:
American Bar Association, Publication Orders
P.O. Box 10892, Chicago, IL 60610

ORDER BY PHONE:
24 hours a day, 7 days a week:
Call 1-800-285-2221 to place a credit card
order. We accept Visa, MasterCard, and
American Express.

EMAIL ORDERS: orders@americanbar.org
FAX ORDERS: 1-312-988-5568

VISIT OUR WEB SITE: www.ShopABA.org
Allow 7-10 days for regular UPS delivery. Need it
sooner? Ask about our overnight delivery options.
Call the ABA Service Center at 1-800-285-2221
for more information.

GUARANTEE:
If—for any reason—you are not satisfied with your
purchase, you may return it within 30 days of
receipt for a refund of the price of the book(s).
No questions asked.

Thank You For Your Order.

Join the ABA Law Practice Division today and receive a substantial discount on Division publications!

Product Code:	Description:	Quantity:	Price:	Total Price:
				$
				$
				$
				$
				$

**Shipping/Handling:		***Tax:**		
$0.00 to $9.99	add $0.00	IL residents add 9.25%	**Subtotal:**	$
$10.00 to $49.99	add $6.95	DC residents add 6%	***Tax:**	$
$50.00 to $99.99	add $8.95		****Shipping/Handling:**	$
$100.00 to $199.99	add $10.95	Yes, I am an ABA member and would like to join the Law Practice Division today! (Add $50.00)		$
$200.00 to $499.99	add $13.95		**Total:**	$